Lotteries for Education

Origins, experiences, lessons

Conall Boyle

IMPRINT ACADEMIC

The moral rights of the author have been asserted. No part of this publication may be reproduced in any form without permission, except for the quotation of brief passages in criticism and discussion.

Published in the UK by Imprint Academic
PO Box 200, Exeter EX5 5YX, UK

Published in the USA by Imprint Academic,
Philosophy Documentation Center PO Box 7147, Charlottesville, VA
22906-7147, USA

ISBN: 978 184540 210 5

A CIP catalogue record for this book is available from the
British Library and US Library of Congress

www.imprint-academic.com

Contents

List of Examples of Lotteries for Educational Places

Non-academically selective lotteries

Academically selective lotteries – mostly universities

Selecting teachers and students by lottery

Introduction

Using a lottery to share out scarce resources has been implemented in various places and times without any clear rationale for its use *being stated or available*. This is equally true in the case of educational lotteries. The recent example of school-places in Brighton came as bolt from the blue to most commentators. The origins of lottery use in this case can be discovered (and will be explained in Chapter 2), but even these originators failed to discover uses from 10 or 20 years earlier which might have set a useful precedent to follow. There is clearly a need for a handbook which would assist those grappling with existing lottery-selection schemes or contemplating implementing them. They could learn from what has gone before as well as understanding the underlying rationale for lottery use.

The main theme of this book is the selection of students for places at schools, colleges and universities. Education is generally a publicly-funded service because the opportunity to learn and gain qualifications is seen as important, especially so as it provides a means of equalising life-chances. There is, rightly, a public interest in how sought-after places at the best schools and colleges are distributed.

One way of ensuring that this is done fairly and efficiently could be through the use of lotteries to award places. What I aim to provide here is a representative collection of examples where this has been done, documenting the evidence and conclusions from these actual cases. This is not an attempt to catalogue every use, nor should the examples thought of as 'exemplars' – ideal models which should be followed. It may be, as Deming (p52 Neave, 1990), that all-wise management guru explained: "Examples teach us nothing unless they are studied with the aid of theory. Most people merely search for examples in order to copy them." I hope that no-one would blindly copy any of the examples given, but there is much that can be learned about what works and what should be avoided. I would hope that educationists, administrators and students of education could gain a better understanding of why lottery allocation was preferred and what those involved in a lottery felt about its use. They can then make an informed decision with more confidence should they wish to implement a similar scheme for themselves.

When documenting the range of lottery allocation schemes that are being used I have tried to find out their context. Who suggested using lotteries in each particular case? How did discussions amongst political groups and legislators lead to lottery use? Where this information is available I will report on it.

Often missing in discussions of public policy are the experiences and views of the public – the very people who are intended to benefit from public services such as education. It is for this reason that I have included many reported comments made when lotteries have been used. These can be found both in print and broadcast media. Views can be found in the form of editorials, but perhaps the most interesting of all are observations made by members of the public who are directly involved in such lottery allocations. These are all opinions, so they are not like the reliable results of opinion polls. But even the ill-informed prejudices of the general public should be heeded because it is they, as voters, who must be satisfied before public policy is changed.

There is an unintended yet powerful consequence of using lotteries to allocate places in education. Analysts can now test some of their cherished theories in proper 'scientific' manner. There is plenty of data available about educational attainment but most of it is of little scientific use because it does not come from properly conducted experiments. Luckily in a few cases where lotteries have been used to decide school- or university-places there is a rare opportunity to do so. Some important questions have been addressed, like: Does choice work? Is there a peer-group effect? Do entry grades predict final degree classification? Gems of validated knowledge can now be extracted from this use of lotteries.

But can it be fair or just to use lotteries to distribute publicly-funded goods? Talk of fairness and justice leads us into the realms of philosophy. I am constantly fascinated and impressed by the arguments of the philosophers but they can sometimes be heavy going! I do not avoid such argumentation altogether in this book: I report one delightful spat between philosophers in Chapter 6. For those who want more of this approach, I include some references for further reading.

My own background as an engineer turned economist leads me towards what the economist Alvin Roth (2002) calls a mechanism-design approach. Using a lottery to distribute prizes is not just an idea, it is also a mechanism. We can reasonably ask: how well does this mechanism work? The influence of experimental psychology, too, is becoming increasingly important, even for economists. The writings of Kahneman & Tversky (1979) should be more influential in understanding the motivations and behaviour of both bureaucrats and applicants. This knowledge does not yet seem to have reached the economists of Public Choice. Economics, psychology and mechanics can thus be combined in order to explain the examples as they are encountered.

A note about rhetorical 'lotteries' from those who should know better: Of course this book is not about lotteries which are used for gambling, but just to put the record straight, here are some examples of 'lotteries' that I will *not* be dealing with:

> **Schools funded in 'postcode lottery'** Education in Wales has turned into a 'postcode lottery' because of changes in the way schools are funded, a government advisor has said. Professor David Reynolds, a senior advisor on education, said divisions between areas were growing as a result of the Welsh Assembly's recent decision to abolish the suggested spending figure for education in Wales. Mr Reynolds is head of the school of education at Exeter University. (BBC 2 Apr 2001)

> **Education "still a lottery"** The gap between the best and worst schools in England is still too wide in spite of significant

improvements in teaching, according to the chief inspector of schools. In his annual report, Chris Woodhead says "the education system remains a 'lottery' in which schools serving similar communities achieve widely varying results". (BBC 9 Feb 1999)

What the word 'lottery' (thankfully used here in quotes) is meant to show in these extracts is that there is an uneven or haphazard distribution of public resources. What I describe in this book is the deliberate use of some form of randomness to decide who wins the prize of a place at an academic establishment. This can be called a lottery, a ballot or even described for what it is – random selection or allocation. Generally the description 'lottery' will be used.

Acknowledgements: I would like to thank Keith Sutherland for agreeing to take on this book, despite his stated "visceral opposition" for the idea of school places by lottery! I think I know what he means, and I doubt if this book will change his mind. Indeed my own conclusions about school-place lotteries are a bit lukewarm (see Chapter 13), although I still think that the Dutch medical school weighted lottery is brilliant and should be emulated throughout university education. I would also like to thank Peter Stone of Stanford university for permission to use an extended extract from one of his papers; Dr Jon Fuller of Queen Mary School of Medicine for a lengthy extract from an article. Ben Willbrink has provided excellent information and comment on the wonderful Dutch medical school lottery. Thanks too to Meike Vernooij for permission to use her photo. I would also like to thank all of the 'Kleroterians', a group of us interested in the practical uses of randomness in social affairs. In particular, Piet Drenth and Martin Wainwright have been very helpful. Your continued interest in the subject has been an inspiration. The Centre for Market and Public Organisation in Bristol has been inspirational; I am especially grateful for their provision of seminars on the topic of school choice, *free of charge* which is a great boon for independent researchers like myself.

Finally, I would like to dedicate this book to the memory of my parents who lived modest lives, mainly because of the need to pay for my education.

Part I:
Lotteries for Non-selective School Places

Chapter 1

School Choice by Lottery?! The 'Choice' Agenda

Brighton says "yes" to a lottery for school places. Brighton is an attractive seaside town on the south coast of England within commuting distance from London. It has its fair share of affluent white-collar workers, but also has a somewhat raffish reputation. There is the exotic pleasure dome erected for the Prince Regent in the 1820s; Brighton is also popular with the gay community and with hippies, a reputation which is enhanced by the swarms of bright young overseas students who flock to the English language schools in the summer. But when the Education Committee of the Brighton & Hove City Council announced at the end of February 2007 that it was going to allocate school places *by lottery* this seemed to come as a bolt from the blue to most people. Parents, many of whom were highly educated and articulate were outraged. There was talk of dark deeds on the Education Committee where the vote was split. Newspapers both local and national expressed their deep distaste for such an unprecedented means of deciding children's futures. Even Professor Anthony O'Hear, the Editor of the journal of the Royal Institute of Philosophy weighed in with strong condemnation.

After much heated argument and debate the Council finally agreed that the strange novelty of a lottery would be used. In all the discussion one fact had seemingly been overlooked by nearly everyone: a lottery for school places was not a new idea at all. It had been widely used in many places in America, and to a lesser extent elsewhere. Lotteries or 'ballots' as they are sometimes coyly called had even been used successfully for many years in the 1980s and 90s in the north of England by the Lancashire local education authority. Just like financial regulators who seem to forget the lessons of the past, so too the educational administrators had forgotten the practical fixes which have worked before.

It was this collective amnesia which prompted me in part to write this book, arising specifically from the Brighton & Hove example, in the hope that administrators do not continually have to 're-invent the wheel'. The Brighton & Hove case sparked off a gratifyingly large amount of comment and discussion which I will draw on extensively. Not all of it is critical; indeed some very thoughtful pieces have appeared in support of the idea of lottery. Perhaps for me as an enthusiast for lottery selection, the best result is that there are now few people in education or elsewhere who are unaware of ballots, lotteries, random selection or whatever they might be called. The fact that they can be a useful administrative tool in resolving difficult school-place decisions is by now also well-known.

The search for such an administrative tool began with the 'comprehensive' ideal. This was the notion that secondary schools should not select entrants on the basis of academic ability. Instead these schools should be open to all, with the local education authorities normally directing children to their nearest school. The next Big Idea that came along was the policy of parental choice. Parents should be allowed to pick whatever school they felt was best for their child. It is inevitable that there will be more applicants than places at some schools. When this happens, what mechanism could be used to decide the winners? A lottery, as we have seen, is one possible answer.

But how did such an idea become policy in a local education authority like Brighton & Hove? Although it arrived at the idea independently, the main impetus towards using lotteries had started at the national government level. I will now describe how this policy evolved. Brighton will not be forgotten, but the details will have to wait until Chapter 3. Here is how the national policy of lottery-use was developed and adopted, and how a think-tank influenced the process:

The National Code for school admission, England[1] 2009

The introduction of a lottery for school-places by Brighton & Hove was only a side-show. Local Education Authorities (LEAs) like Brighton & Hove have always had responsibility for implementing school admissions policies, but they are constrained by central government, which lays down the rules of the game. These rules take the form of Codes and derive from the deliberations of a parliamentary committee which includes school choice in its remit.

The Education and Skills Committee of the House of Commons (since 2007 it has become the Children, Schools and Families Committee) sits on an on-going basis to discuss various educational topics. During its 2003-4 session, its deliberations first mention the use of lotteries for school admissions. This is what the Report of the Education and Skills Committee (2004) said (p48)

Admission by lottery?
Since we completed our evidence-taking, proposals have emerged for a school admission system based on a lottery. These proposals, most notably from a commission on the issue set up by the Social Market Foundation, set out a new approach which breaks the link between address and admissions. The system enables parents to express a preference for up to six schools, without regard to local authority boundaries, with school places allocated without reference to the family's address. Where schools are oversubscribed places would be assigned by means of a ballot where all parents had an equal chance of success. The proposal permits appeals but only on the grounds of maladministration.

At first glance this proposal offers an enticing opportunity to end the dominance of those with the resources to buy homes near to the school of their choice or to influence the outcome of the admissions

---

[1] Yes, *England*. Education is a devolved responsibility for the other parts of the United Kingdom – Scotland, Wales and Northern Ireland.

system by other means. However, given the evidence from the DfES which highlighted parents' desire for certainty and predictability in the school admissions system it is not clear to us that parents would welcome an approach that increased the level of uncertainty in the system.

It appears to us that there is more work to be done in considering how the admissions lottery approach would affect different groups of children and their families. In particular we are conscious that costs related to school transport can be considerable. Unless school transport can be publicly financed, the impact of failing to get a place at the nearest school will disproportionately burden poorer families. For similar reasons it may be necessary to modify the lottery system for rural areas in order to ensure that children were not required to travel unreasonable distances to attend school. Further consideration is also needed on how siblings, children with special needs, and casual admissions would be handled.

A footnote to this Report adds: "The report of the Social Market Foundation's Commission on school admissions is as yet unpublished. We are grateful for advice from the Social Market Foundation on their proposals."

Notice how the parliamentarians have picked up on several of the main points about the use of lottery for school admissions: It offers "an enticing opportunity to end the dominance of those with the resources to buy homes near to the school of their choice", which clearly vexes the committee members. I will be looking at the evidence for the 'good school house-price effect' in Chapter 3.

But the parliamentarians are still wary of the parents, who value "certainty and predictability in the school admissions system". The costs of transporting children further afield are also a concern. Although the house-price effect of good schools and the parental acceptability of lottery selection will feature repeatedly in the wider debates over admissions, transport costs come up less often. It is good to see that someone is keeping an eye on the cost implications of enticing policies like lottery selection.

The (re)birth of an idea: the Social Market Foundation Report:
There had been earlier rumblings suggesting a lottery for school
places, but which had little impact. For example, Alan Smithers,
one of the country's leading educational researchers had suggested
in *Times Educational Supplement* (12 Jan 1996) that all children
should obtain a certificate of readiness for secondary education.
Then parents could apply to any school they wish. If a school
received too many applications then all its places should be
randomly allocated. Harry Brighouse made a similar but less
detailed proposal in *The Independent* (8 Jun 2000) noting that
lotteries were already in use in the US in Milwaukee. He also
warned that crafty schools might try to 'pick the pool' from which
their applicants would be drawn.

The Social Market Foundation had established a
'Commission on School Choice' in 2003, although it was really no
more than an internal discussion group. It was their *Report on
Schools Admissions* (Haddad, July 2004) that produced the
considered case for lottery selection, which as we saw convinced
the relevant parliamentary committee to seriously consider
adopting it.

The Social Market Foundation (SMF) is a British public
policy think-tank which aims to promote and produce policies
supporting the 'social market'. This was the concept of the SMF's
first publication, published in 1989, in which former chair, Robert
Skidelsky argued that: "The use of the phrase 'social market
economy' signifies a choice in favour of market economy. It means
that we turn to the market economy that is, above all, one which is
embedded in social arrangements regarded as 'fair' as a first resort
and the government as a last resort, not the other way round."
Although popular with John Major's Conservative government in
the 1990s, the SMF has since moved closer to the Labour Party and
was associated with some of the policies of Blair and Brown's New
Labour, particularly on issues of public service reform. (from
Wikipedia)

The main conclusion of the SMF Report on School
Admissions is that "The Commission supports a system of

increased choice and resolution of oversubscription by ballot, believing that it will not only produce desired outcomes, but will also be a system that can be seen to be fair by parents." Note that for the SMF it is a belief, not a finding supported by evidence that parental choice mediated by a lottery will produce the outcomes which are desired. Later, in Chapter 4, I will report on some of the academics who have investigated the thorny issue of choice and whether it works or not. Just as contentious is the suggestion that parents would see lottery selection as fair, a conclusion which is disputed by many editorials, but again which will be tested against the evidence in Chapter 2.

There are a number of different values (objectives) that could, in principle, says the SMF Report, govern the design of admissions criteria for schools. These are: allowing parental choice, raising educational attainment, decreasing social segregation, rejecting academic selection and encouraging localism. However,

> The Commission recognises two fundamental problems in ranking these values through admissions arrangements. First, as has been seen, rules designed to rank these values are in practice very much open to abuse by more privileged parents (and in some cases by schools). Second, even addressing this question in the abstract, the Commission itself feels unable to rank these values, and certainly to rank them in a way that would be deemed fair by all parties. We therefore support the notion of *procedural fairness* as a second best solution, which the Commission feels is the best response to a situation of reasonable and insuperable value pluralism. ... A school admissions ballot is therefore favoured, for oversubscribed places.

To say, as the SMF puts it, that using lotteries is a 'second best solution' is hardly a ringing endorsement, and it could well be misunderstood. But to place 'procedural fairness' above these values required some heavyweight academic support. They quote Oberholzer & al (1997) who say that:

> Random decision mechanisms are the embodiment of fair allocation procedures. None of the personal characteristics that typically interfere with decision processes in a completely unwarranted way enter procedures based on chance: Nepotism is out of the question.

The rich and the powerful do not have any better chances than the poor and the humble if allocation relies on random decision processes.

These are just some of the many reasons why a lottery (or a random decision process as Oberholzer describe it) could be used to decide school admissions. I will return to this form of philosophical argumentation in Chapter 5, and look at a wider range of reasons for and against the use of lotteries for school places.

The Report of the SMF Commission goes on to explain why lottery selection would be good for *schools*, too:

A system in which choice takes precedence and conflicting choices are resolved by a single oversubscription criterion [i.e. a lottery] that is fair between all parents has the virtue of preventing schools from engaging in selection. It therefore drives them to compete for pupils on the basis of teaching quality, rather than using pupil selection to improve their own outcomes at the expense of overall educational attainment. Such a system can embody several values. In preventing schools selecting pupils, and offering children of any social class equal prospects of being admitted to any given school, it should lead to less social segregation, without social mixing driving the system. And given that the prospects of disadvantaged children attending better schools will be enhanced, there will also be favourable social justice implications.

The government response: The Parliamentary Committee for education may make proposals, as it did in July 2004 on the use of lotteries in school admissions, but it is up to the government to make the laws which turn proposals into directives. In November 2004, in response to the Report by MPs on Secondary Education: School Admissions (described above) the Government echoed many of their comments on the use of lotteries:

Admission by lottery?: There is more work to be done in considering how the admissions lottery approach would affect different groups of children and their families. Costs related to school transport can be considerable. Unless school transport can be publicly financed, the impact of failing to get a place at the nearest school will disproportionately burden poorer families. It would be necessary to look at local patterns of application and admission and travel to school routes before any assessment could be soundly based. The Government wants parents to be able to assess their chances of getting a place at a preferred school. That would not be possible under a total lottery system.

So the principle of the lottery seems to be accepted, but the cost of transport needs to be thought through. Again a reassuring reminder that our legislators think carefully before committing tax-revenues.

Towards the final version of the Code: The *School Admissions Code – Draft Skeleton* was published (DfES 2006) by the government in April 2006. There are 11 selection criteria which are expressly *forbidden*, plus several more which are deemed poor practice. The draft Code then suggests, somewhat obliquely, that a lottery can be used: Paragraph 2.33 of the Code states:

> If admission authorities decide to use random allocation when schools are oversubscribed, they need to set out clearly how this will be operated. They should undertake a fresh round of random allocation when deciding who should be offered a place from a waiting list, and should not use the results of an earlier round of random allocation. Such an approach would disadvantage those who had applied for a place at the school after the first random allocation was carried out. Some admission authorities have used random allocation as a final tie-breaker, or after other acceptable and fair criteria have been used.

There are no other reference in the document to 'random allocation'. The question of "an earlier round" which appears here is not elaborated.

The final version of the School Admission Code: minor but crucial amendments: I reproduce the relevant paragraphs of the draft School Admissions Code which was published on February

28, 2007 by the DfES. I have included the final amendments, which illustrate some of the thought-processes around at the time.

2.33 Random allocation of school places can be good practice particularly for urban areas and secondary schools. However, it may not be suitable in rural areas. It may be used as the sole means of allocating places or alongside other oversubscription criteria.(~~such as a 'tie break'~~) Random allocation can widen access to schools for those unable to afford to buy houses near to favoured schools and create greater social equity.

2.34 If admission authorities decide to use random allocation when schools are oversubscribed, they need to set out clearly how this will operate, and **must** ensure that arrangements are transparent. They **must** (~~should~~) undertake a fresh round of random allocation when deciding which child is to be offered a place from a waiting list, and **must** (~~should~~) **not** use the results of an earlier round of random allocation as this would disadvantage those who had applied for a place at the school after the first random allocation was carried out.

2.35 In order to provide verification that the random allocation process has been carried out fairly, admission authorities **should** ensure that they are supervised by someone independent of the school.

Note that two 'should's have been strengthened to 'must's from previous draft (My emphases)

And so it was that in a Written Ministerial Statement to the House of Commons on Thursday, 4th December 2008 The Secretary of State for Children, Schools and Families Ed Balls said:

Today I have presented to Parliament the revised school admissions code [*School Admissions Code 2009 Edition* (DCSF 2009)] and school admission appeals code. Subject to the parliamentary procedure, these codes will come into force in February 2009. Through the Education and Skills Act 2008 we have strengthened the statutory admissions framework to ensure that all schools adopt fair and lawful admissions practices. Local authorities have an important role to monitor compliance with the code and are now required to report annually to the schools adjudicator on the fairness and legality of the admission arrangements for all schools in their area. As the independent enforcer of fair access to schools, schools adjudicators now have a wider remit to consider any admission arrangements that come to their attention in addition to any complaints received through an objection. The schools adjudicator will report annually to the Secretary of State on how fair access is being achieved locally.

The Schools Adjudicator We will hear much more from the Schools Adjudicator in later chapters, so this may be a useful point to explain how this independent office was established and how it functions. The Office of the Schools Adjudicator was set up in 1999 by a Parliamentary Act. The Schools Adjudicator's functions include determining between objections to school admission arrangements. Parents "can object to any aspect of a school's admission arrangements which is unlawful or does not comply with the mandatory provisions of the School Admissions Code, that is those requirements or provisions which the Code states **'must'** or **'must not'** be complied with." Local authorities too, as well as governing bodies of schools can also object. Following an investigation the Adjudicator will issue a 'decision'. Unless this is challenged, it then becomes mandatory for the parties involved. "The adjudicator's decision is final and must be implemented immediately. It can only be challenged by application to the high court for judicial review." (based on *www.schoolsadjudicator. gov.uk/index.cfm*)

Comment: How to run a proper lottery: The last two paragraphs of the Code (2.34, 2.35 above) show that someone at the Department has spotted the pitfalls as well as the benefits of using random allocation. These circumstances surrounding any lottery which admits or rejects candidates may become highly contentious. Just saying "we used a lottery, you lost" will not be enough. To avoid any hint of discrimination the lottery draw may be held at a ceremony open to all. If not, how can any candidate be sure that the draw was not rigged? A lottery draw leaves no evidence, no audit trail, only results. To ensure the widest acceptance of the results, perhaps it would be best to call in an independent outside scrutineer. I set out my recommendations for 'practical lotteries' in full in Chapter 12.

The Theory of Public Choice and the Choice Agenda

So far in this chapter you have encountered what has happened. For the second part, in common with most of the chapters in this book, I will look at some of the theory or evidence which informs the examples or decisions taken from the first part of the chapter. For example, what was it that led the Social Market Foundation to *believe* (their word) that increased parental choice together with lotteries would deliver the desired outcome of better schools? We have seen how the education system for England adopted a policy of using lotteries. Now, in the second half of this chapter, I would like to explain the theory behind this.

It was parental choice and the inevitable over-subscription at the best schools which was the main mover behind the use of lotteries. Even if parents were given no choice and their children were directed to a particular school, then there *might* be some reason to have recourse to the use of lotteries, but it is unlikely. To put it bluntly: If there was no parental choice then there would hardly be any need for lotteries. Abolish choice and lotteries could go too. Many of those who complain about the damnable novelty of lottery-choosing are really hankering for a time when it was the schools which chose pupils, generally on the basis of academic achievement, or even ability to pay.

In the following sections I explain how choice by schools transformed into parental choice:

No choice: Your child will be schooled: Universal compulsory state-funded education: All children are compelled to go to school in developed states the world over. There are many good reasons for this, not least because it provides an opportunity for all citizens to better themselves through education. This education is provided free of charge by taxpayer-funded authorities, but at which school? In UK parlance compulsory schooling is provided at Primary level for children aged 5 to 10, and Secondary level from 11 to 16 or whatever is the school-leaving age. After the age of 16 education is variegated, with post-18 education considered as 'Higher'. Only at this point is education optional. Since you do not have to attend higher education, then the way selection works at this stage is bound to be different. Entry into higher education will be dealt with in the second Part of this book. My focus in this first Part is on the school system, focussing mainly the transition from primary to secondary schooling, because this is where lotteries are likely to be used in deciding who goes to which school.

There is a rich variety of schooling modes, such as the private fee-paying schools, confusingly called 'public schools' in the UK. There can be a religious dimensions to schooling, as well as home-based non-institutionalised education. There are some schools which use the label 'independent', usually to show that they are free of state control either at the local or state level. Some may be 'opted-out' of local authority control, some may be fee-paying. However, many of these schools rely in great part on public funds, and all are subject to some forms of inspection. All must operate within the laws of the land.

How schools used to choose their pupils (and sometimes still do): In the old days, before universal compulsory state-funded secondary education life was much simpler. You only went to school if your parents could pay, or maybe if you were very clever, you could win a scholarship. Even so, some schools were more highly rated than others, so 'rationing-by-queuing' developed. Schools maintained waiting lists and you had to register your child's name to be considered. For the well-off it may have been a matter of 'putting Nigel's name down for Eton' as soon as he was born. Even if Nigel was sufficiently high up the list when the time came for his entry, the school could still impose further tests, such as examinations or interviews. Another curious form of prioritisation which I recall from my youth in Dublin was based on fatherhood: you would only be considered for a sought-after boys' school if your father had also attended.

Rationing by priority on a waiting list is an age-old technique, sometimes called First-Come-First-Served, and is recognised as a standard and fair method when a business cannot serve all of its customers at once. Some economists such as Taylor et al. (2003) have studied this and suggested that a lottery would be both a fairer and more efficient method of dealing with customers. Many schools, particularly at the primary level still maintain waiting lists for places. Perhaps they too should consider replacing this system by a lottery. (A few already do, as will be seen later).

There may also be a physical cost involved in waiting in a queue: we regularly see pictures of fans camping out over-night at Wimbledon to get hold of tickets for the Final. It is something of a surprise to discover the same thing can happen for school places. In Belgium, according to Cantillon (2009), in order to get their child into their preferred school, parents will queue up at that school, sleeping in camper vans for days if necessary! It could be said that this form of queuing is democratic, that it favours no-one, and it is egalitarian in that rich and poor alike spend their own time in order to capture the prize. Since rich people value their own time more highly than the poor then the cost/reward ratio in queuing favours the less well-off.

Schools may arrange entry based on academic tests. Perhaps the system which has been most widely used in England and Wales was the '11-plus'. This was a straight-forward intelligence (IQ) test, and a residual version of it is still in use in parts of England. Selecting school entrants by IQ and no other criterion is a good example of a meritocratic system. It has many attractive features. I will return to the theme of 'meritocracy' later in Chapter 7. But it was the negative reaction to this division of children into 'winners' and 'failures' at the age of 11 on the basis of an IQ test that led to the abandonment of academic selection in most of England and all of Wales. Instead schools were to be local, admitting children of all abilities; in other words 'comprehensive'.

Comprehensive schooling: No choice but the local school. In a few parts of England some elements of academic selection remain, but generally, and this includes Brighton & Hove, the comprehensives reign. For these schools no entry tests are allowed. Being a lot bigger than primary schools the comprehensives will draw pupils from a wider catchment area. Priority for entry was normally based on distance from the school.

A similar system operates throughout the US, but no special label is needed for these public (free, funded by taxes) local schools. A particular problem which bedevils schooling in the US is that of racial segregation. Because neighbourhoods are racially segregated this can lead to schools which are also divided by race. The solution adopted included that of bussing of students to different parts of the school district. This was not voluntary; schools were obliged to accept whoever was sent, although students may have had some choice of school.

So far, all the methods of selecting students for admission to secondary school have involved choice by the schools or by the local authority. But the change which eventually led to selection by lottery was of course parental choice. Before explaining how this worked, I want to look at how the idea of 'choice' has come to dominate school entry. The theory comes in two parts: First there is the economists' version, known as the Theory of Public Choice; secondly is the Choice Agenda which derives from Theory of Public Choice, but is also a product of sociology and politics.

The Theory of Public Choice: The economists' Theory of Public Choice is their explanation for some of the mechanisms at work in public-sector organisations like schools: because schools are not run like profit-oriented businesses the normal rules of the market do not apply.

In the school business you will not find customers (parents) choosing which product (school place) to purchase, making their decision to purchase on the basis of the quality of the product (educational package on offer). Nor are there producers (schools) tailoring their product to what the market demands, trimming costs to keep up with the competition, and selling their products to all comers at the market price. Instead there are bureaucrats (head-teachers, governors) who choose which children to accept into the school, by whatever means they choose. Should you trust the professionalism of these bureaucrats to choose pupils solely on educational grounds, children who in their expert judgement would be the ones most likely to benefit from the teaching and learning on offer at their school?

The highly influential economists who developed the Theory of Public Choice will have none of this (James M Buchanan[2] and Gordon Tullock are the main protagonists). They would say that these bureaucrats are just like any other economic actor, be they buyers or sellers; they just want to maximise the benefits for themselves. In the case of the head-teacher in a state school that probably means he or she would prefer to pick the brightest students in order to improve the examination results of the school. S/he would also like to pick well-behaved students who will be less burdensome. The easiest way to achieve this desirable result is of course to pick children from middle-class families. The parents too, wish to maximise their return from schooling which is free at the point of use. By getting their child into a 'better' school they enhance that child's life chances at no extra cost. Economists have an expression for this activity of extracting a benefit from goods paid for by others (usually the state): it is called 'rent-seeking'.

In the competition for school places, the 'best' schools are the ones that parents most wish to get their children into. The best schools may have achieved that status by improving the quality of teaching and discipline, or it may just be the result of the catchment area from which the school entry is drawn. When schools are compelled to recruit only within a limited local area, or if they are the only school in the area, the incentive for the school to improve is, in the eyes of the Public-Choice economists non-existent.

---

[2] A good general introduction to the topic can be found in **Buchanan, James M** (2003) *What is Public Choice Theory?* lecture given on 2nd Feb 2003 at Hillsdale College from *http://www.hillsdale.edu/imprimis/ 2003/march/default.htm*

But theirs is a strongly economistic agenda, part of the neo-conservative market liberalisation movement which has gripped governments since the 1980s. Their ideal solution would be the total privatisation of schools, as suggested by Friedman (1995). Significant moves in this direction have already been made in the US. I will deal with the much touted gimmick of school-vouchers in Chapter 4.

For most politicians, though this is a step too far. They wish to drive education (and other publicly funded services) in a more market-oriented direction, and are looking for answers. 'Choice' seems to be the favoured answer. But why should choice produce better schools? The theory derives from free-market economics which predicts that producers competing against each other will work hard to improve their products and take market share from each other. The weakest will go out of business, the best will thrive and expand.

You may find this characterisation of schoolteachers as selfish maximisers to be repugnant; you may know, or may even be a dedicated hard-working teacher who chose a career in education from a wish to be of service. Many teachers will have accepted the lower pay in return for the satisfaction of giving those less fortunate a better chance in life. The public choice economists are challenged by behavioural economists like Frank (2004) and Fehr (2001) who have shown that the caricature of the single-minded greedy economic man is not valid in either the commercial or especially in the not-for-profit sectors. Real people have a wider range of motivations beyond self-interest. Treating employees as if they are greedy self-interested maximisers, for example by using performance bonuses, causes them to act in this way, often, as we have seen in financial services to the great detriment of their employer and of society at large. Little of this impinges on policy makers, who as Keynes once famously put it "are slaves of a defunct economist".

The Choice Agenda Choice for the customers[3] who make use of public services is widely seen as a way of improving them. You may not agree with the market-derived idea that choosy customers will drive up the standards of educational achievement in schools, but both the new-Labour Blair government and its Conservative opponents certainly do. Giving patients and parents the right to choose who treats their ailments or teaches their children is seen a effective politically and administratively. 'Choice' is coming, whether you like it or not! The consequences of choice in taxpayer-funded services is fairly obvious: Provided for free at the point of consumption, there is bound to be an excess of demand for the best clinics or schools, compared to the supply available. If the market does not ration the scarce places, some other means has to be found.

The case that forcing a kind of pseudo-market onto schools will improve educational standards is often assumed to be self-evident, an obvious consequence of simple economic theory. Some evidence to support the Choice Agenda comes from Julian Le Grand, a policy wonk favoured by the Blair government. He laid out the case for 'Choice' in an LSE lecture (LeGrand 2006). His evidence that "choice works" is mainly based on opinion polling. In surveys, the working class seem to warm to the idea of choice much more than the middle classes. Choice therefore must be egalitarian.

It is easy to see the political attraction of the choice agenda, but does it really drive up standards? I will return to this theme in Chapter 4, where the results of lottery use provides the scientific evidence that it almost certainly does not. Nevertheless 'choice' remains a powerful political slogan.

Parental choice comes to the comprehensives: When British educational policy changed to allow parents the choice of any

---

[3] I recall that from the early days of the Thatcher administration there was a deliberate move to ensure that pupils, patients and passengers would henceforth be referred to as 'customers' in order to inculcate free-market virtues into public sector employees.

school in the borough there was the inevitable over-subscription for the 'best' schools. Some method to adjudicate between the competing claims had to be found. One technique was to tacitly allow these 'best' schools to cherry-pick the pupils who were the best, brightest and easiest to teach. Schools would do this for their own convenience, and in order to maintain the league-table rankings of the school. To economists of the Theory of Public Choice this comes as no surprise – administrators, driven by self-interest will always act to make life easier for themselves.

A further problem is "the sharp elbows of the middle classes". As Le Grand puts it: "by virtue of their education, articulacy, and general self-confidence, the middle class are simply better at persuading", and grabbing the best places. Seemingly egalitarian moves like extra testing, interviews and reports just reinforce these problems.

It was in order to thwart the machinations of the school head-teachers, and to prevent parental choice degenerating into a sham that extra rules were bolted on to procedures. These outlawed interviews, questions about parents' jobs or marital status or previous school results or references. Eventually as we have seen, when these strictures did not seem to be working, the UK Parliament decreed in 2007 that a lottery might well be used. Almost certainly selecting school entrants by lottery would never have come about were it not for the widespread political support for the parental-Choice Agenda.

Chapter 2

Lotteries for Places at a School: What do Parents Think?

Throughout this book I will be looking at a wide variety of examples of lottery use in different educational settings. This chapter deals with examples of **single schools** where a lottery is used as part of the process which decides who to admit or reject. The next chapter will look at borough-wide school-place lotteries which involve many schools in a clearing-house mechanism.

As with most of the chapters in this book, after the examples the second half of the chapter looks at some inferences – validated knowledge which relates to the first half. In this chapter it is the psychological aspects of lottery that will be examined. It is said that parents have very negative *feelings* about their children's fate being decided by the luck of the draw. But is this true? Only a properly conducted public opinion survey could test these feelings, and fortunately one exists. But first let's look at a few examples where lotteries are being used as part of the admissions process by single schools.

Examples of schools in England using a lottery:

Only schools which have some control over their admissions procedures could contemplate using a lottery. The process should be quite simple: parents apply to such a school and it is the school which can, if it so decides, run a single lottery to decide who to admit. Of course there will be questions of eligibility – who is entitled to apply – but these can be sorted out after the draw.

Among the details of these examples you will also hear about the emotional turmoil which the choice agenda creates and how the lottery can affect those involved.

(1) Lancashire LEA: A forgotten example from the 1990s: The first English borough to use a lottery for school places was not Brighton & Hove. Forgotten it seems by all the commentators and administrators was the example of the Lancashire Local Education Authority (LEA) in the 1990s. This did not affect the whole of the LEA, just two schools within it. One of these was in Burnley; the other was in Ormskirk. Both towns had several schools, and it was the town not the entire County which was the catchment area for each. The two schools involved were Habergham High School in Burnley and Ormskirk Grammar School (but non-selective; it retained Grammar in its title until 2001 when it merged with another school). Both were heavily over-subscribed, and both had been using ballots (lotteries) to decide entry. "The Lancashire County Council scheme divides the town [Burnley] into four areas so that children from each one have an equal chance to enter the popular former grammar school. A similar scheme is operated for two other Lancashire schools, in Ormskirk." (*The Independent*, Jun 2, 1994)

The mechanics of how the Lancashire LEA ran the lottery is explained as: "Children with brothers and sisters at the 1,114-pupil Habergham school are guaranteed places, and two or three are admitted on medical or social grounds. The application forms for the remaining 100 or so of the 173 places are shuffled and numbered by one council official while another reads out the numbers from random selection tables drawn up by computer." (*The Independent*, Jun 5, 1994)

By 1994 this method of selection had been in use for 13 years. It was then challenged by five parents whose children had been denied entry (*The Independent*, July 28, 1994). At first the parents were successful: John Patten, the then Conservative education minister upheld their complaint. When asked in

Parliament if he proposed to end the allocation of secondary school places by random selection, he replied that he

> has made it clear that he does not consider random selection to be an appropriate way of allocating school places. It is, however, for local education authorities to determine arrangements for admission to county and voluntary controlled schools. I understand that Lancashire LEA has decided to consult parents and others on a proposal that the use of random selection for admission to schools in Burnley and Ormskirk be discontinued. (Hansard *HC Deb Jun 14, 1994*)

Later this was reinforced with a government Circular (*DfEE 6/93*) which ruled against lottery selection. But that was not the end of the story. The LEA appealed to the High Court. The parents lost. Mr Justice MacPherson ruled that lottery selection was "lawful and fair" (*The Independent*, July 28, 1994). The High Court had became involved because in those times that was the formal avenue of appeal against admissions decisions. It was not until 1999 that the Office of the Schools Adjudicator was established.

Why did Burnley and Ormskirk use the lottery? Both schools are "near the top of the academic league tables" (*The Independent*, Jul 28, 1994). David Clayton, Habergham's (Burnley) headmaster, said: "If we became a neighbourhood comprehensive that would infuriate the parents living on the other side of town. Short of becoming academically selective again, there is no neat solution to the problem." (*The Independent*, May 11, 1994) There was also a quote about using the lottery from Tony Richardson, the head of Ormskirk school: "In the abstract it has appeal but when it comes to individual children and families it can be very distressing." (*Guardian* Jan 1, 1996)

To find out more about this unusual example of the use of lottery selection, I carried out some primary research of my own. In a telephone interview in 1996 with Terry Clarke an official involved at Lancashire County Hall, he confirmed that the lottery was still available for use for Habergham High School, Burnley, but it had not actually been used in 1995 because there were fewer applicants. He had no knowledge of how it started, or if it was in use elsewhere. I was interested to know some more about this draw, so asked Mr Clarke how and when the draw was actually carried out. He explained that the draw is done in secret, with even the actual day of the draw kept secret lest there be a rush of parents. It had been proposed that one or two scrutineers could be invited to view the process to confirm it is above board. No photos of the draw are available, nor would they be in future.

There are very few comments from parents about the process. One parent who was reported as saying "They are using bingo-style lotteries to allocate places. I believe they are acting against Government guidelines"(*The Independent*, May 12, 1994), which merely states what was going on. Much later, in 2007 I received some comment from Martin Wainwright on the day that the Brighton & Hove story broke. Martin is Northern Editor of the Guardian, and also had a piece in Comment is Free in *The Guardian* (Mar 1, 2007) about lotteries on that day. His email included this information:

> The scheme was never wildly popular but was accepted (rightly) as the fairest solution. It is no longer used because of changes to both schools and their pupil numbers. Incidentally, I was making some calls about this yesterday in my Guardian role and the Lancashire experience has been almost completely forgotten, even by Lancashire county council which had to do quite some digging to check on the details. The Department for Education and Skills was aware, but not in much detail. The BBC and others said Brighton & Hove was a first. We thus had a mainly hypothetical discussion in the media about an idea which has already been tested – and indeed subjected to judicial review in 1994 after some Burnley parents objected. The review upheld the scheme.

(2) Eastwood School, Essex 2000, 2005. This is an example of a curious spat between three foundation schools in Essex, England. In 2000 Eastwood school in Leigh-on-sea faced a challenge to its lottery entry procedure from two other local Foundation schools – King Edmund and FitzWimarc. These two schools had taken their complaint to the Schools Adjudicator, and it is from his Reports

(ADA/00118 and ADA/00125) that these details are drawn. All three schools are comprehensive – open to all — but there are still 10 Grammar Schools with selective entry in the Essex local authority. Eastwood School specialises in sports and wished to give parents from a wide area a chance to enter their child there. When there were more applicants than places Eastwood implemented a lottery. The other local foundations objected that this involved creaming off students from their catchment area. The allocation of places at random across the wider priority area is, they said "totally unacceptable. It is just a front for a selection process. The draw has no means of being authenticated, validated or audited."

Eastwood countered that:

> The use of random allocation for offering places to pupils from outside the priority catchment area was chosen to allow the school to continue to take pupils from all its traditional feeder primary schools rather than restricting admissions to pupils from the nearest schools. Advice was taken from DfEE (Department *for* Education) and the arrangements were based on the Lancashire model which had been tested in court.

The school gave details of their procedure for the random allocation of places in the case of oversubscription. This involves the allocation of an electronically generated random number to each applicant and then sorting the applications into numerical order.

The Adjudicator ruled that:

> The allocation of places at random (or by lot) is controversial… but the school have explained their reasons for adopting this procedure, namely to take account of the views of feeder primary schools and to give parents from the whole of their catchment area an equal chance rather than using geographical distance from the school. No evidence has been submitted demonstrating that the arrangement is unfair or unclear to parents. The allocation procedure has been explained in detail and is a straightforward and open random process. ..... I cannot uphold the objections to this aspect of the arrangements. Given the feelings of concern that allocating places at random can arouse, the school may wish to consider reviewing the policy from time to time

with a view to ensuring that it continues to enjoy the full confidence
of parents.

So the case was dismissed; a lottery is indeed acceptable both in
general terms and in the specific example given. The Adjudicator
also referred to "Similar [lottery-based] procedures [that] have
worked satisfactorily elsewhere for a number of years." (that is
before 2000). Both he and Eastwood School mention the example in
Lancashire, so the Adjudicator, the Department for Education and
framers of the School's entry procedures were well aware of this
example long before the Brighton lottery story broke. I can find no
instance of this case figuring in national or local media.

*Again in 2005 there was an objection to the random selection of students
by Eastwood. Again the Adjudicator found it acceptable:* This time it
was a local authority, Southend-on-Sea Borough Council acting on
behalf of local parents who took their case to the Schools
Adjudicator (Case *ADA000731*). The Council felt that the random
basis for allocation of places was not clear for parents. No
indication is given, they said, of how the process is operated and
the parents find it difficult to estimate their chances of being
offered a place.

Eastwood school responded that The Social Market
Foundation had recommended a random system for admissions
(details of this were given in Chapter 1) and the idea has been
supported by a number of other bodies. The system is
administered fairly using a computer programme for the random
selection of names. It is a system that has been in operation for
some years and parents have a clear idea how it works. The present
situation had arisen because of the success and increased
popularity of the school and some difficulties being experienced in
neighbouring schools, they claimed.

The Adjudicator gave guarded approval to random
selection in the following terms:

> I recommend that the school and the Council set out on a re-
> organisation of [the local schools] as soon as possible. In making this
> recommendation, I should make clear that I do not suggest that the
> school needs to abandon some use of an element of random selection.

Random selection (like all other methods of allocating school places) has advantages and disadvantages. The main advantage is that it provides schools with a good social mix of children from families who live in different areas of a town. The main disadvantage is that some children are not allocated in schools very near their homes and have to travel some distance to the school where they are allocated places. It is for the schools in the area, the admission forum and the Council to decide on these matters. They should, however, avoid a situation in which a small group of parents in the town is treated differently from everyone else.

Again it is curious to see the easy acceptance of random selection by the Adjudicator. There was no objection to a lottery as such, only the lack of information about the procedure that was available to parents. Eastwood School showed that they are well informed about precedents for lottery use. One might quibble with their over-reliance on the magic of computers to intimidate the opposition. Phrases like "electronically generated random number" may be valid, but do not in themselves make the process more or less sound.

That the system was still in operation in 2008 as is shown by the reported complaint of Kirstie Williams, of Eastwood, an 11-year-old who lives just 328 yards from the secondary school of her choice, Eastwood. She had lost out in the lottery. In an editorial in the local newspaper *Essex Echo* (Apr 4, 2008):

> **School Lottery is Unfair** While there is inevitably a lottery element to the allocation system, it should make allowances for young people in Kirstie's situation. The message from the authorities is "tough luck". The education system should not be in the business of creating innocent victims, children whose secondary education is undermined before it has even begun.

The Editor seems unaware that this really *is* a lottery. Perhaps he is right though, to bring up the fact that this technique has a rough edge to it and cannot always be defended as rational, even if, as the Adjudicator explains, it treats all of the parents in the feeder area equally.

(3) St. Bernadette's RC Primary School, Brighton 2004: It may come as a surprise to learn that a lottery had already been successfully used to decide entrants to a school in Brighton. This was three years before the headlines announced the (by now) notorious Brighton & Hove city-wide lottery for secondary school places. (Details of this in the next chapter, as example 11.)

The decision by St. Bernadette's primary school to select entrants by lottery seems to have been a co-operative effort between the school governors and the Schools Adjudicator. According to a report in *The Independent* (Oct 25, 2004): "The school's governors decided something needed to be done after it became clear the school could be swamped with a wave of applications for next year. With just 30 new entrants a year, there is a huge demand for places." The decision to use a lottery was approved by the Schools Adjudicator in these terms: "This is an unfortunate situation but it seems to be the fairest way. Although the drawing of lots is unusual, it is acceptable in exceptional circumstances." The governors had preferred a distance-based criterion but were urged by the Adjudicator to explore the use of a lottery for the next round of admissions.

Being faith-based, St Bernadette's has a scale of priorities for admission according to how keenly the families practise their religion. Currently (in 2009) the school prospectus (*www.stbernadettes.org.uk*) still indicates that "In the event of all else being equal, the school will draw lots, under the scrutiny of an independent LA admissions officer." Another RC Primary in Brighton, Cottesmore St Mary's is also reported in *The (Brighton) Argus* (May 20, 2009) to have introduced a lottery for entrants. No hint of controversy about these lotteries can be found in either the local or the national newspapers.

(4) Haberdashers' Aske's Hatcham Academy, London 2005: If the spat between three schools in Essex passed off with little media attention the same cannot be said for Haberdashers' Aske's, which hit the news with their quite modest lottery scheme in September

2005. The name – Haberdashers' Aske's – is a nightmare for those who have difficulty with apostrophes, so it's HA from now on!

There are several schools with the HA name, the best-known of which is the independent fee-paying HA Boys School, now at Elstree, previously at trendy Hampstead, North London. Perhaps because of the association of haberdashery and the Jewish community (as well as its location in North-West London), the school is popular with Jewish parents, as the glittering list of old boys shows. It includes Simon Schama the historian and Sacha Baron Cohen ('Borat'); the play/film *The History Boys* is thought to have been based on HABS (from *Wikipedia*). The HA Hatcham City Academy School has a somewhat less glittering list of old-boys and old-girls, but is highly sought-after nonetheless.

In September, 2005 HA Hatcham College in Lewisham, south London, became an Academy. It is, according to a report in the *Independent* (Sept 29, 2005) "one of the most popular schools in the country, with 2,500 parents chasing just 208 places." As a result, the college intended to adopt a lottery-based admissions system to avoid social segregation at the school. It is re-assuring to see that "The names of the successful are selected randomly by an outside independent body", which shows that the school is aware of the possible pitfalls of leaving the draw to some mysterious computer-generated random numbers. The report goes on "The 'random allocation' scheme – similar to lotteries already run by some oversubscribed schools in the US – is seen as a way of bringing a halt to the process of wealthier parents buying up properties near a popular school." (Note that in 2005 reporters still had to put 'random allocation' in quotes.)

In a later report in the *Independent* (Oct 2, 2005) it was claimed that "The lottery is being pioneered [*sic*] by Haberdashers' Aske's". So they were aware of similar schemes in the US, but not it seems either in nearby Essex or in Lancashire. The BBC were better informed (*BBC News, Sept 29, 2005*) stating that this is "one of a number of schools now allocating some of its places to children in the area on a random basis." It went on to explain that "About half of the places were allocated to children with special needs, children in care, siblings of existing pupils [this is the normal practice] and to the 10 percent of the whole intake selected on musical aptitude. Of the remaining places, half were allocated on proximity to the school, while the other half were selected at random from within the school's three-mile catchment area."

Comments on this scheme came from high and low: One local family, the Neilsons who lived just 600 metres from the school, complained when their son lost out in the lottery: "I strongly disagree with the new approach of random allocation. It shows that children's future is now a lottery to the education authority." The BBC news item received a small number of on-line comments, most of which were favourable. The one negative suggestion from Charani of Somerset was that "It leaves too much in doubt.... children should be allocated places on a first come, first served basis only." A keen advocate of the age-old British custom of queuing there then!

A more weighty comment came from Martin Rogers, of the Education Network, an independent body which advises local councils. He believes the policy will be good for education and society:

> It is a welcome attempt to break the stranglehold of the better-off on the most over-subscribed schools. It's not a healthy trend that society is increasingly segregated, whether by wealth, class or religion. There could also potentially be major educational gains as a number of people who might not have expected to get in will be able to. The families of those they displace might then take more interest in other schools in the area.

The view of an official spokesman at the DfEE (Ministry of Education) was reported to be that "Haberdashers' Aske's has decided to use random allocation, which can be popular with parents because it's not subjective and gives an equal opportunity of admission."

Perhaps the oddest commentary was to be found in the editorial columns of *The Independent on Sunday* (Oct 2, 2005):

> **The schools lottery is an admission of failure**, [A] fundamental problem is that *parents are unlikely to accept the legitimacy of a system*

based, in effect, on the roll of a dice. [my emphasis] This is not simply because they are irrationally committed to the fate of their children, unable to appreciate the purity of a perfectly fair system for the allocation of a scarce resource. It is because people prefer a system based on hypocrisy – where at least they can see the iniquities – to one based on luck. While a lottery is theoretically a fairer way to allocate oversubscribed places than any other, it deprives parents of some ability to plan ahead, and takes what small degree of control they have out of their hands.

Strong words indeed! When editorials talk of 'legitimacy' and 'hypocrisy' then something serious is amiss. Perhaps they are right, that the natural human aversion to the clean-cut mechanism of lottery is so strong that a messy decision is more acceptable. John Elster (1989) advocated as much in child custody cases. Where a judge could not decide between two warring parents over which of them should be the main custodian, his advice to the judge is: toss a coin *in secret* to decide, but give the parents some rational-sounding explanation for the decision. I have always found this advice to be deeply disturbing, but others may be able to see the common sense of it.

Even more oddly, by the following Thursday (Oct 6, 2005) an editorial in the same paper, *The Independent* proclaimed that

A lottery is the way forward, Parents may frown on the idea of a lottery because they attach such importance to getting their children into the school of their choice. And geography may appear more rational than luck as a criterion. However, there is every reason to believe that the random allocation of places, as it is officially called, is fairer than the system it replaces. Allocating places according to geography meant that richer parents were able to snap them up by buying a house close to the school. Property values around popular schools rose as a result. A lottery would end that.

Confused? At the end of this chapter I report on an excellent opinion poll survey which tries to answer this basic question: school place lotteries — can parents get to accept them as legitimate, non-hypocritical and fair?

So how did the HA scheme pan out? In 2007 when the story of Brighton & Hove school-place lottery broke, a reporter, Sian Griffiths, from *The Times* (Mar 1, 2007) took the initiative of finding out about this earlier example. She discovered that the lottery selection scheme was still in operation but with some modifications:

> Half of the places at the Haberdashers' schools are allocated to children living in the inner catchment area, roughly within half a mile of the school. The remaining places are randomly allocated via an electronic sorting machine to families living within a three-mile radius of each school. ... the system ensured that each school had pupils from a mix of social backgrounds.

The reason for this two-tiered system were spelled out by Dr Sidwell, who is the Director of the HA Foundation as follows:

> "We wanted to keep a diverse intake as we felt it was important to the ethos of the schools, which are both in fairly disadvantaged areas. ... By imposing a three-mile radius for the random allocation we ensure we also take in children from less advantaged parts of Peckham."

But what of the overall reaction by the parents to the lottery scheme? Dr Sidwell continued:

> "Unlike the Brighton lottery scheme, the random allocation admissions system operated by the Haberdashers' schools has not caused controversy. Parents have understood it and see it as very fair. We do have appeals, but they are not because of the lottery. They are usually where parents are querying the distance they live from the school or where they feel we haven't checked the special needs of their child properly, as we give priority to special needs children."

This is *most* encouraging, especially for advocates of lottery selection like myself.

But alas, it did not last. Despite the positive reactions by parents and others described by Dr Sidwell, the Haberdashers' Aske's entry lottery is no more. In the 2009 prospectus the school states that admissions criteria have changed, and random allocation is no longer used. Instead, they have reverted to a proximity measure, awarding places to those who live nearest, after other categories like siblings have been satisfied. "The intake is fully comprehensive and we are oversubscribed in all nine of our ability bands. We operate a Banding Policy as required by the Admissions Code of Practice" (that would be the English Code explained in Chapter 1). What they now employ is not lottery but what could be called a 'banding and proximity admissions criterion'. I will examine banding by ability as an alternative or an adjunct to lottery selection later in Chapter 5.

(5) Lady Margaret Girls' School, London 2007: This example is of interest because it involves a faith-based school. It also highlights the fact that decisions based on proximity are open to fraud by over-ambitious parents. A report on *BBC News* (April 19, 2007) explains

> **Top girls' school adopts lottery** A popular girls' comprehensive school in London which was criticised over its admissions system has decided to allocate some places by lottery. Lady Margaret School in Parson's Green had to pay compensation to two families after the [Adjudicator] upheld their complaints. The voluntary aided Church of England school will now allocate 50 places to regular church-goers and 40 by lottery. Parents' representatives say the move reflects a worrying trend. Lady Margaret School is heavily over-subscribed with 600 applicants for the 90 places it allocates to 11-year-olds every September. The [Adjudicator] had ruled [Case ADA1136] that the school did not deal with admissions applications objectively and fairly, [because they conducted interviews with some applicants.]

The Chairman of the governors, Richard Waterhouse, said the admissions system had been revised in line with the new national guidelines, which say random allocation is an acceptable method of dealing with over-subscription. He explained that there were few alternatives.

> "When you sweep away the previous criteria, and you aren't allowed to take primary school references and estimated parental support, you are left with all criteria focused on distance. We realised that if we did it on distance we would have people arguing about the system we used. We were also getting fraudulent addresses, people renting a flat next door and getting a household bill. So we decided to go for

random allocation. The lottery places will be limited generally to children from the Hammersmith and Fulham area, but pupils in a few other areas with good transport links to the school will also be eligible."

In his Report, the Adjudicator addressed the specifics of using a lottery at a faith-based Christian school:

In considering the appropriateness of a faith school using random allocation I have taken into account the response from the diocese. It is the diocese's view that the process can be explained clearly and transparently, it is equitable and no more inappropriate for a Church school than any other school wishing to ensure equality of access. If the voluntary aided school thinks a lottery is suitable and the diocese thinks it appropriate, and there appear to be no grounds on which to reject it, I am of the view that this part of the objection should not be upheld.

There was a time, 400 years ago, when *any* use of a lottery to decide matters was considered ungodly, a profane and unwarranted calling down of the Almighty. If you want to know more about this view, and the robust rejection of it see Gataker's *The Nature and Uses of Lotteries. (1627, reissued 2008)* It is good to know that the diocesan authorities do not object to lotteries on religious or moral grounds these days!

Some further details of the exact procedure emerge from the Adjudicator's report. This is not a simple lottery with 600 girls applying for one of the 90 places available, which would mean that there could be six or seven girls competing for each place. Instead girls are assigned to one of 12 groups determined by which of three ability bands, two catchment areas and foundation or open they fall into before being allocated by lot. The Adjudicator commented that "This seems to me to make it impossible for any parent to have a reasonable idea of their chances of success".

So the school seems to be running 12 separate lotteries. The Adjudicator thinks that parents should know which group their girl is in and what chance she stands within that group. The school disagrees: "The order of events is: application – testing – sorting by hand – random selection. There are complications, but largely for those administering the system, not the parent!" The Adjudicator rejected this argument, telling the school that they should provide more information so that parents can calculate exactly what chance of success they face.

As well as being baffling, this information might in turn spark off some strategic behaviour by the more astute parents. If it appears that there are a large number of very bright, high-scoring girls applying, that could reduce the chances of entry for such girls. Parents who got wind of this fact could instruct their daughter to fake it, to deliberately do badly in the test in order to be classified with the less-crowded low-scoring group. This would improve that girl's chances of entry. I will return to this aspect of strategic behaviour in a later chapter. Here it remains a reminder that designing mechanisms for allocating school places should be fair and workable, but they must also contend with those who wish to get around the system by fair means or foul.

This risk is not hypothetical. When a case of 'home address fraud' was discovered, an editorial in *The Times* (Jul 4, 2009) suggested that lotteries could prevent such anti-social behaviour. The fraud concerned a parent who had been caught out pretending to live at an address in the catchment area of a sought-after primary school which uses proximity as the sole entry criterion. The *Times* editorial advocated the abolition of catchment areas, with parents free to choose any primary school. There would then be no incentive to lie about home addresses. If there were more applicants than places at any school, then "the allocation should be settled by lottery. Precisely because a lottery is blind, it is fair. Everyone, regardless of income or background, has exactly the same chance of success." It is gratifying to see the easy acceptance of lotteries for school places by 2009, especially when compared to the controversy it had caused two years earlier when the Brighton & Hove school-place lottery was revealed.

Lotteries for single schools: Outside England:

(6) Michael J Petrides School, New York 1994, 1998: An editorial in the *New York Times* (Mar 10, 1998) declaimed:

> **A School Lottery Gone Wrong** The Petrides School was supposed to be a flagship experimental school serving the entire district of Staten Island. The school's lavish facilities and 42 acres of grounds, which once housed the College of Staten Island, were transferred to the public school system in 1994. The plan was to offer kindergarten through 12th grade, with emphasis on technology and languages. The promise made to the community by district officials was that the school would be open to all, with a computerized, random lottery to determine admission.

The school was popular. There were 653 applications for 93 places, and selection was supposed to be by a lottery run by the school. Following an inquiry it was discovered that 30 percent of the students were children of school system employees. Public confidence in the lottery system was shattered. The Principal of the school was suspended, although no wrong-doing was proven.

> Missing records made it hard to retrace the lottery process and to prove that any laws or school board regulations had been broken. But the investigators say they are not convinced that any lottery was conducted for the current school year. But favoritism in student selection is utterly poisonous to public trust.

This example shows that it is not just the principle of using random selection that needs to be argued, the practicalities of the process must be right too. I will return to these practicalities in Chapter 12.

(7) SEED Boarding School, Baltimore Maryland US 2008: (Report by Thomas L Friedman *New York Times*, May 25, 2008). Here is a heart-warming example which judging by the language used and the reported reactions of the participants, educational opportunities in parts of the US must be pretty dire, and any chance of escape must seem highly desirable. Compared to the highly equivocal views of parents in the UK, or more correctly, the views *ascribed* to parents by newspaper editors, it is refreshing to see an example where nothing but positive feelings are recorded:

SEED (it's not clear what 'SEED' stands for) is a publicly funded boarding school which was about to admit its first 80 students, the vast majority of whom are African-American and from the most disadvantaged and violent school districts. As the reporter eulogised:

> Every once in a while as a journalist you see a scene that grips you and will not let go, a scene that is at once so uplifting and so cruel it's difficult to even convey in words.

> SEED Maryland got more than 300 applications for 80 places. The families all crowded into the Notre Dame auditorium, clutching their lottery numbers like rosaries. [note the mixing-in of religious imagery] Each applicant was assigned a number, which was written on one of these balls. Eighty were picked for the public school, 40 for the wait list. On stage, there were two of those cages they use in church-sponsored bingo games. Each ping-pong ball bore the lottery number of a student applicant. One by one, a lottery volunteer would crank the bingo cage, a ping-pong ball would roll out, the number would be read and someone in the audience would shriek with joy, while everyone else slumped just a little bit lower. One fewer place left ...

One might ask if this is just a cruel spectacle, or is it indeed a necessary procedure which ensures this primitive draw using ping-pong balls is carried out properly? At least the victims can see their fate being sealed, unlike many mysterious computer-generated random number generators used elsewhere. It was not really necessary to be in attendance. Later on, those who had won were notified in the usual way. Again, more high-blown emotions are recorded: "We called one school counselor the next day and told her that so-and-so was chosen," said the administrator, "and she said: "Thank you. You have just saved this child's life."

Another report from Tanika White in the *Baltimore Sun* (May 18, 2008) on the same event records similar high-flown emotions:

"This is the answer to a prayer," said a joyous Evelyn Collins of Randallstown, just after her grandson's number was called. His was the third number announced, but Nos. 1 and 2 were not in the audience to squeal the way Collins did or jump and wave like her grandson, Lucas Gutierrez, did. …….. Jumping, yelping, cheering and hugging were in no short supply yesterday during the first few minutes of the lottery. But midway through, other activities became more prevalent: hand-holding, rocking, foot-tapping and, all throughout the too-warm auditorium, silent praying. Carolyn Tenai of Lansdowne and her son Elijah Anthony Johnson Jr. clasped hands and put their heads together, willing the lottery ball with No. 91 to free itself from the pack. "If we get it," Tenai vowed, "I'll probably pass out on the floor……"

Even the fate of the losers was not overlooked

For many other families, the day ended less happily. Maurice Chandler [left work early]..so his son, Maurice Jr., his wife, Malinda, and their two other children …could all be a part of the process. They sat together in a row, quietly, listening for No. 17. But once the first class was selected and the priority wait list called, the auditorium seats began to empty without Maurice's number being uttered. The 11-year-old hid his face in his shirt, leaned against his father's arm and cried. His mother tried to reassure everyone that Maurice's future still was bright. "I know whatever he does, he's going to succeed," she said. But Maurice was inconsolable. "It was a long shot," said his father, his eyes heavy from lack of sleep. "But it was a chance we had to take."

Oh dear! Maurice Jr. has had to cope with a major set-back in his life at the tender age of 11. This story is a poignant reminder of the damage to the feelings of students and their families that may accompany any selection process, not just a lottery. Administrators may just see names and numbers on computer screens, but there is a living breathing human being behind each number. We would all like to think, even the protagonists of the Theory of Public Choice that public services exist to make life better for the service users. Part of that quality of service should include paying heed to the feelings of the users and the fairness of the processes used to grant or deny such public services.

(8) Federal City College, Washington DC 1969: This is, I believe, a unique example of a community college accepting students without any pre-qualifications. Normally some form of screening would apply but in this case because of a sudden rush of students for a newly opening college only a lottery was used. Selection on the basis of grades or test scores was seen as inappropriate for the institution was intended to be an 'open door' community college. Wolfle (1970) who reported on this was highly critical:

> The use of a lottery to decide who will receive a benefit that cannot be granted to all .. it is a denial of rationality.... To choose students by a random process is to deny the ability of the faculty to select those applicants who show greatest promise or who appear most likely to benefit from higher education... Should Judgment wear a blindfold, or should she be required to see the persons judged?

He is quite right when he says that the use of a lottery precludes rationality. His faith in the ability of the faculty select may, however be misplaced. And the last time I looked 'Judgment' did indeed wear a blindfold (see graphic on p216). Perhaps the least objectionable feature of this process was that it was one-off. In later years normal selection methods were employed.

(9) Daewon International School, Korea 2008: (from *Joongang Daily* Dec 27, 2008): This report contains some nice details (as well as a picture of ecstatic winners):

> **Fate of international middle school hopefuls decided by ping-pong balls** At 11 a.m. yesterday at Daewon Middle School in Gwangjin District, eastern Seoul, a lottery took place to select the final students to be admitted into the institution, which will be newly opened as an international school in March next year. The more than 350 students who gathered in the hall drew ping-pong balls of orange, white and green, and then sat in chairs arranged in rows behind color-coded signposts.

So yet again primitive technology is being used, but at least it is easy to see and understand.

At 12:40 p.m. when Kim Il-hyung, the school's principal, stepped forward to draw an orange-colored ball, students and family members sitting behind the orange-colored post shrieked with joy. Those holding white and green balls lamented over their misfortune. Of 366 kids who passed an interview process to be able to participate in yesterday's lottery, 138 who drew orange ping-pong balls can now enter Daewon International School. Younghoon Middle School, the other international middle school that will open next March, selected 160 new students from 475 applicants through the same method. .... The Seoul Metropolitan Office of Education came up with the lottery system to quell the criticism raised by groups such as the Korean Teachers and Education Workers Union that the schools are only for privileged students..... .

This lottery system also brought down the usual condemnation. An editorial in the same paper says that

The victims are the students. It was distressing to see hardworking, intelligent young students forced to accept rejection after working hard at their studies. ..... The selection of students should be left to the discretion of the international middle schools. Schools know best how to pick qualified and talented students.

(10) CAPE Primary School, Camarillo, California 2009: Kindergarten (primary) school places at the Camarillo Academy of Progressive Education (CAPE) in California are allocated by a lottery. As a public school (that is state-funded in the US) , CAPE cannot charge tuition and it may not discriminate in its enrolment process. First availability for classroom space in the 2009-10 school year goes to current CAPE students and their siblings with the remaining spaces filled by a lottery which will be held in March (*www.CamarilloCharter.org*).

Scotland, too may be moving towards the use of lotteries to decide entry to popular primary schools. In 2008 it was reported that East Renfrewshire Council was considering introducing the ballot system for one heavily over-subscribed school, Mearns Primary to decide the primary-one intake for August that year. (*The Scotsman*, May 6, 2008). No reports of a ballot actually happening can be found subsequently, so maybe it was just an idle threat.

Measuring public opinion:
Parental feelings about school place lotteries

In this second part of the chapter I move on from describing actual schemes where a lottery decides who wins the school-place and who is rejected. Now I want to consider what valid inferences can be drawn about the psychological reactions of the participants, especially the parents who are involved in this process. Comments in the media have often been hostile, reporting that some parents and pupils think a lottery is "unfair". Editorials have been inconsistent, sometimes branding lotteries "illegitimate" and never acceptable to parents; yet others have seen the logic of the scheme. Administrators like the head of Haberdashers' Aske's may claim that "parents have understood [the need for lotteries] and see it as very fair". The reports from Baltimore in the US and Korea depict lottery-victims as being in a high state of euphoria or dejection.

But none of this is proper evidence. The high emotions encountered at lottery drawings may just be another aspect of our 'reality-TV' culture. Claims in editorials or by head-teachers need to be substantiated before being accepted especially when they are contradictory – and there will be many more contradictory claims to be drawn from the examples in this book.

Fortunately there has been a reliable study of public opinion on the use of lotteries for school places. This is a survey from the Sutton Trust which tackles the question of lottery use for school places head on, but in an appropriate context.

Sutton Trust survey of public opinion on lotteries for school-places: According to *Wikipedia* Sir Peter Lampl founded the Sutton Trust to improve educational opportunities for young people from non-privileged backgrounds and to increase social mobility. The trust funds a variety of research, campaigning and philanthropic projects including the 'Open Access' experiment which funds 70 percent of places at the academically selective Belvedere School in Liverpool. The Sutton Trust is that rare gem — an organisation which is both independent of government and academia and has funds to commission research. Its agenda seems to be oriented towards the betterment of educational opportunity for all.

I had recognised in my own researches (Boyle, 2006) that there was a need for an opinion survey to test the views of the public especially the parents on the acceptability of school choice by lottery. This was answered in the form of an imaginative, informative and well-funded piece of independent research which was carried out by the Sutton Trust in 2007. In their report *Ballots in school admissions* (Sutton Trust, 2007) they surveyed the use of ballots (lotteries) for school places in various countries.

As the Sutton Trust report explains, one striking contrast between England and the US is that the lotteries which feature in the allocation of school places are seldom commented on in the US, whereas editorials in the UK (as we have seen) often wax indignant about them. Why the difference? Is it familiarity, or perhaps a deeper democratic urge in the US that makes the self-evident fairness of the use of lotteries more acceptable? The report suggests that the topic has not been investigated by researchers overseas because it is seen as a non-issue. When asked, US academics report that as far as they are aware the US public believe that random allocation of school places ('seats' in US jargon) is self-evidently fair and practical and that it has the seal of approval of the public at large as a transparent way of deciding who wins the school places when schools are oversubscribed. As with the example of student housing lotteries in the US (in Chapter 10) I too have been surprised by this lack of academic interest. This is not because academics are unaware of it; I will make use several papers, mostly American which take advantage of the 'natural experiment' provided by lottery allocations of school places and student housing, but none comment on the merits of the lottery itself.

So how should places in over-subscribed schools be decided? The opinion poll findings are the most significant part of the Report from the Sutton Trust. They commissioned Ipsos MORI to gauge the views of the public in the UK on what are the fairest ways of allocating places at over-subscribed schools. The survey was carried out in late March 2007, which was shortly *after* the story broke that Brighton was to use lottery allocation. The following is a summary of findings from the a survey: Interviews had been undertaken with a representative cross-section of 1,928 adults, so would have included many parents. There were three significant questions (significant to the present enquiry anyway) relating to the fairness or unfairness of school admissions decisions:

Question 1 gave a range of eight different options to decide who gets in to an over-subscribed school:

The options were: *(in order of fairness, as seen by the respondents)*

1. Priority to children who live closer to the school
2. Priority to children with brother/sister already at the school
3. Sharing places equally between children who fall into different ability bands
4. Priority to children who do better in a test or exam
5. Sharing places equally between children whose families fall into different income bands
6. Following an interview with the headteacher/another teacher
7. *Randomly allocating places (a ballot or a lottery)*
8. Giving priority to children of a certain religion or faith

The responses are listed in order of 'fairness' as perceived by the respondents. Proximity – those living nearest the school was seen as the fairest option. The most unfair decider was judged to be selection by religious faith. A ballot or lottery was considered to be the second most unfair method. Little comfort for lottery enthusiasts there! The reports warns that

A high proportion of respondents (between 40% and 70%) were unable to describe any of the methods of allocating school places as either fair or unfair, indicating both that the issue of school admissions is complex – one criterion may be fair in one context, but not in another – and that many may feel they do not understand the issues sufficiently to make a judgment.

The option which caused the most uncertainty was No. 5 on banding by income, which is not the same as banding by ability. Few people would be familiar with either form of banding. As we have seen, banding by ability, not income, has emerged as a strong alternative to the use of lotteries, for example at Haberdashers' Aske's (4) and Lady Margaret School (5).

Question 2 was more subtle: Here it is in full:

Scenario: A community comprehensive school has 100 places on offer, but 200 families have applied for these places. All of the families live within 2 miles of the school. The school first gives places to children with special educational needs and those with a brother or sister already at the school.

> *Q. In your opinion, which is the fairer way of deciding*
> *which children get a place at the school?*

+++ 35%   1. By choosing the families whose

children live nearest to the school

++ 32%   2. By a ballot

+ 17%   3. Neither

16%   4. Don't know

(% figures are the responses. I've added +++ to illustrate strength of response)

This shows quite a turnaround in opinion! In this somewhat contrived example there are just two options: proximity or a lottery. The results show little difference in preference between the two. Respondents can now see the benefits of ballots/lotteries, despite having strong reservations before.

Question 3 pushes the respondents a bit further: (again here is the full question):

Scenario: A Christian faith secondary school has 100 places on offer, but 200 families have applied for these places. All of the families have been going to church regularly for at least two years. The school first gives places to children with special educational needs and those with a brother or sister already at the school.

> Q. *In your opinion, which is the fairer way of deciding which*
>
> *children get a place at the school?*

+ 20%   1. By judging which of the families are the

   most committed to the Christian faith

+++ 36%   2. By a ballot

++ 25%   3. Neither

18%   (Don't know)

Turning lottery sceptics into enthusiasts is quite a feat, but it has been done here. Bravo to the Sutton Trust for exploring these 'scenarios', which show that with a pause for reflection and with the question framed appropriately, then the public and parents in particular can come to accept and maybe even approve of lottery selection and allocation.

Conclusion: Generally when asked straight out in a survey: "Should school places be handed out by lottery?" the answer is a resounding 'No!' (There is a similar result when a lottery for university places is suggested, as will be seen in Chapter 6.) It is only when the use of lotteries is 'framed' – given an appropriate setting – that respondents can bring themselves to accept the idea of random selection. This shift from outright rejection of lottery allocation to grudging acceptance of the practice needs some explanation.

Perhaps the first hurdle in the acceptance of lotteries for school places is the description 'lottery', which conjures up so many negative associations. The first thing that springs to mind might be gambling at casinos or even the fairly anodyne National Lottery. Newspaper headlines bang on about the 'post-code lotteries' which deny you medical treatment. Crazed gunmen are said to kill people 'at random'. Who would want these things to happen to their children? Lottery suffers from such a poor image that when it is used for school-place allocation, then it is sometimes disguised by being called a 'ballot' or as the English Code prefers to put it: 'random allocation', having deliberately struck out the word 'lottery' in the final draft.

As well as the negative image foisted on lotteries by the media, there is also the element of unfamiliarity, especially for the public in the UK who have had little experience of using lotteries to decide serious matters like school places. Proper scientific analyses of public opinion may not always give reliable answers but they are better by far than the descriptions of depression and euphoria caused by lottery choosing which are alleged by commentators. There is evidence that parents will re-act negatively to school-place lotteries, preferring instead proximity as a fairer method. However, once the issues have been narrowed down and explained then proximity and lottery emerge as equally acceptable for school-place choosing.

Chapter 3

School-place Lotteries in a Borough: House-price Effects

School places across the borough or district: The clearing-house model

The last chapter dealt with single schools which operate their own admissions policy. When Local Education Authorities (in the UK) or School Districts (in the US) administer many schools at either primary or secondary level then applications for multiple schools may be required. Again this is a consequence of the parental choice agenda. Parents are encouraged to indicate their preferences based on whatever information they can command. The Authority then acts as the clearing agent, matching the supply of school-places with the 'demand' from the parents. It is this role as the intermediary agent, and the need for parents to list schools in order of preference that marks out this process as different to the single school application process in the last chapter.

Examples of school-place lotteries in English boroughs

(11) Brighton & Hove LEA 2007: This example was introduced at the start of Chapter 1, but now is the chance to fill in the details of the process by which Brighton & Hove Council made its decision. It must have been a slow news day on February 28, 2007 when the *Press Association (PA)* posted the story that there was to be a

> **Council lottery for school places:** A Labour-run council has become the first in England to choose to run a lottery for places at popular

schools to stop middle-class parents dominating the best
Secondaries.......

The story caught fire, appeared in the national dailies, and was
reported from as far a-field as Australia. The *PA* report went on:

Brighton and Hove is believed to be the first council in England to
decide to use the new lottery option after ministers reformed the
school admissions code. The new code, which comes into force on
Wednesday, advises schools that lotteries are a good way to allocate
places fairly when popular schools are oversubscribed. Parents are
invited to choose their favoured schools in order of preference but
many Secondaries attract far more applications than they have places
available. Ministers proposed the lottery option as a way to loosen
the grip of middle-class parents on the best state schools. For years
affluent parents have paid their way into the best schools by buying
increasingly expensive houses within catchment areas.

There is some confusion in this news item. Of course this was not
the first time that a lottery was used by an LEA. We have already
seen the example (1) of Burnley and Ormskirk in Lancashire. Nor
did Brighton & Hove's decision result from any new government
directive. Although it was true that Parliament and the Department
of Education was finalising its Admissions Code (see Chapter 1 for
details) in 2007, it was not due to come into operation until 2009.
Brighton & Hove had been developing its own scheme for some
time. They may well have been aware of the discussions going on
in Parliament, but it was their own decision to use a lottery, not
central government's.

The trigger for this move was Brighton & Hove's proposal
in 2004 to alter the school catchment areas and also bring in some
element of parental choice. In a letter to the *Brighton Argus* (the
local paper) on Nov 23, 2006 a Mr Graeme Kerr suggested because
of the new catchment areas "the only fair system would be for the
council to remove the notion of freedom of choice altogether and
allocate school places on a lottery system. At least then every child
would have an equal chance of getting the school of their choice."
This is the first time the local newspaper records a mention of
school choice by lottery. By December, according to the *Argus,*

parents had received proposals of changed catchment areas together with the use of a 'lottery' in cases of oversubscription. As seems typical with all such changes, parents were reported to be "united in their opposition". A local Action Group (see *www.schools4communities.co.uk*) had been set up to spread the news, but their main gripe seemed to be about catchments, not lotteries.

By January 6, 2007 Brighton parents were sufficiently incensed to stage a 300-person demonstration and 3,000-name petition against the proposals, but again this was mainly about catchment areas. It was only at the end of this news item that *The Argus* noted that "..where a popular school was oversubscribed, a 'luck of the draw' electronic lottery system would be used to decide which pupils got priority". In a photo in the report a child can be seen carrying a placard saying *"Education is not a Lottery"*.

By February 2nd the Schools sub-Committee of the Council had narrowly approved the new plans, but by a "knife-edge vote" and with stories of dark deeds needed to win the vote. After further re-consideration, the schools committee gave the final clear-cut go-ahead on the 27th. All through this process, catchment areas not lotteries had been the main bone of contention with parents, but that's not the way the rest of the world saw it.

The following day (Feb 28, 2007) some national newspapers reported the factual aspects of the story: "Council lottery for school places" (*Daily Mail*) and "Brighton school places to be picked by lottery" in *The Times*, which had also picked up on the fact that Brighton was Labour-run. By March 1st the story had developed legs. Reports could be found in papers world-wide, but now the tone had changed from factual to opinionated: for *The Times* it was "Parents' fury as lottery decides which pupils get best state places", picking up on the local protest; *The Financial Times* took an oddly different angle "Move to allocate school places by lottery counters choice agenda"; *The Telegraph* seemed slow to catch up; the headline "School places lottery will hit house prices" did not appear until March 3rd, two days later.

By the weekend (Mar 4, 2007) the editorials and commentators were weighing in. In the *Independent* it was "Parents

Need Choice, Not Luck", for the *Observer* it was "Give Children a Chance, Not a Lottery", and the *Sunday Times* claimed "It's Simple: Be Unfair and Schools Get Better". The right-leaning *Sunday Telegraph* took a political line "Tories attack council's plan to allocate school places by lottery".

That did not completely exhaust the controversy surrounding the Brighton & Hove lottery. Parents took the case to the Adjudicator (ADA/001077 July, 2007). He backed the use of lotteries to allocate school places (or "ballots" as he is still calling them), although again it was catchment areas which were the main gripe of the protesting parents.

Later experience with the use of lotteries emerged from a Report by the Schools Adjudicator in August 2009: Brighton & Hove continue to include random allocation in their admission arrangements for all secondary schools. However, for admissions in 2009, only four schools actually used it. Controversy over the use of random allocation has been minimal at secondary school appeal hearings. There has been little focus on the issue of random allocation, apart from those who live very close to the more popular schools. Overall, parents have accepted the change in a relatively short time.

(12) Hertfordshire and other English LEAs, 2007: After the story broke that Labour-controlled Brighton & Hove was about to use school-place lotteries, newspapers started to discover that there were more lotteries already in use in other parts of England. Norfolk LEA confirmed that it too, was looking into a version of the lottery system for its 372 primary and secondary schools which could be in operation by the following autumn. North Somerset council had also written a lottery system into its admissions procedures for its 78 primary and secondary schools and Dorset county council is using one for 102 of its secondary schools for the first time next year. (*The Guardian* March 3, 2007)

Hertfordshire LEA produced the most detailed information about their use of lotteries. According to a report in *The Guardian* (March 2, 2007) they decided to introduce an electronic random ballot *(sic)* for admission to its single-sex schools, where traditionally there have been far more applicants than places. Since this was a Tory-run council that seemed to take the political steam out of the argument to some extent. There are some interesting quotes from Hertfordshire which claims that the lottery is the fairest way to decide who wins a place at its most popular schools, despite the fact many parents are said to think differently.

> "People are wrong to claim we are abdicating responsibility as we are trying to bring a fairer access to more children. Some parents claim that families living on the side of a village nearest a school had an unfair advantage when criteria were based on distance. With a lottery all have an equal chance of winning a place. We have more than 12,000 applicants for school places each year and 80 percent of pupils get their first choice and 90 percent one of the three they name. Parents can still appeal against a decision. We are using the lottery system and will see how it goes". (*BBC News*, Mar 5, 2007)

In another piece in *The Guardian* (Mar 1, 2007) about the Hertfordshire lottery selection process an alternative view was heard from a school-teacher: Alan Gray who is a head-teacher in St Albans said:

> "I believe very passionately that schools should serve their locality, and ideally I would like every local school to be a good school. I would hate the idea that somebody around the corner from my school failed to get in because of a lottery system and that the place went instead to somebody living five miles away."

So far the problem of what to do when good schools are over-subscribed has *not* included the obvious solution: make all schools good schools, so well done to Mr Gray for saying this! How to do it is another question altogether which I will not attempt to address.

A later Report by the Schools Adjudicator in 2009 showed how the use of lotteries developed in Hertfordshire. The report includes a claim that random allocation was introduced as a direct result of parental pressure under the fair access agenda. It is still used for allocation by the seven community single sex schools, but only for certain categories of applicant. In all, 497 pupils were allocated by lottery, which was a mere 2 percent of all allocations in the area. Hertfordshire LEA comments that no significant level of concern over lottery use has been officially raised or noted in any survey or feedback process.

Examples of lottery allocation of school-places in the US

There are very many examples to be found in the US, but the use of a lottery is usually incidental to the main objectives of specific schemes. Whereas the effect on house prices is the dominant issue in England, in the US de-segregation seems to be the main driver. Earlier ideas of achieving racial mixing involved the bussing of students to different parts of the school district. 'Bussing' acquired a bad name but the objective of racial mixing remains. The following examples are included to illustrate a particular point.

Testing whether 'parental choice' works: (13) Chicago Public Schools 1980s onwards: A paper by Cullen, Jacob and Levitt (2003) explains that school choice came to Chicago in response to a 1980 de-segregation decree. The goal was to create schools whose racial composition roughly matched the racial composition of the school system. More than half of all high-school students have made use of the choice option rather than attend their local school. Students must submit an application to the school of their choice; if the number of applicants exceeds the number of available positions, lotteries are used to determine the allocation places at that school. The reason for more than one lottery at each school is explained as:

> There are explicit rules governing the way in which the lotteries are conducted. Because of desegregation goals and variation in the number of available slots at different grade levels, separate lotteries are conducted for each gender-race-grade combination. Thus a particular school may also conduct several separate lotteries.

These rules constitute a form of 'weighted lottery'. Confusingly the same description will be used for the Dutch medical school entry lottery, where weighting is purely on grades. Here in Chicago because of classification by race and gender there will be separate lotteries for each.

I will be returning to this example of school-choice by lottery from Chicago in the next chapter because it makes a major contribution to the 'parental choice' debate. The use of lotteries provides an elegant opportunity to carry out a proper scientific test on the efficacy of the choice agenda.

Weighting by class and race: (14) Pasadena School District, California 1999: This is similar to the previous scheme in Chicago. The explanation given to parents is interesting and includes:

> .. in 2002 the district decided to embark on a three-year plan to create a more equitable, predictable, and transparent placement system by utilizing a weighted computerized lottery system. The first school-wide computerized sample lottery system prototype was built by a programmer who was also an active parent on a school site council. Socio-economic statistics of the applicant pool are compared to the district's student population overall. If the applicant pool percentages are not comparable to district percentages, the district uses a mathematical formula to award more lottery numbers to the underrepresented group to maintain balanced attendance in the magnet schools. For example, in 2008–09, 52 percent of the district's students qualified for free lunch but only 40 percent of the applicant pool for a particular grade level qualified. In such an instance, those applicants may receive extra lottery numbers. The district may also award extra numbers to maintain a balance between students who live within the city limits and those who do not. (*www.buildingchoice.org*)

Does this tinkering with the mechanism of the lottery in the cause of racial and class equalisation arouse any objections? So far I have found no adverse comment on this.

Parental Choice can lead to re-segregation: (15) Charlotte-Mecklenburg School District, North Carolina 2002. Charlotte-Mecklenburg public school district (CMS) had been operating a race-based student assignment plan ('bussing') for three decades. In 2001 they were ordered to introduce parental choice instead. In the spring of 2002 parents were asked to submit their top three choices of school for each child. Approximately one third of the schools in the district were oversubscribed with admission being determined by a lottery system.

The details of the scheme show some of the complexities that arise when lottery allocation is used:

> Students who list a given school as their first choice were sorted by priority group and a randomly assigned lottery number. The random number was assigned by a computer using an algorithm that was said to be verified with CMS computer programmers. Parents do not know their lottery numbers at the time of submitting their choice forms. Slots were then assigned in order of priority group and random number. If a school was not filled by those who had listed it as a first choice, the lottery would repeat the process with those listing the school as a second choice, using the same priority groups as above. For most oversubscribed schools, seats were filled by the time the second choices came up (Hastings et al, 2006).

Another paper based on the North Carolina experience points out one of the ironic consequences of giving parents choice. According to Bifulco & Ladd (2007) this was to *re*-segregate the schools to some extent. This of course ran counter to the earlier policy of de-segregation which allocated students to different schools based on their racial complexion. There is evidence "from countries around the world that when parents are empowered to choose schools, education systems tend to be more segregated by race and socio-economic status than would be the case without parental choice" according to Bifulco & Ladd. The fact that this choice was mediated by lottery means that it can be taken to be the true preference of the parents and cannot easily be dismissed as an effect of racial discrimination.

True believers never give up: (16) Charter Schools, Newark NJ 2009. *The Economist* is a fervent believer in free-market solutions. I include this item to show how the belief in market-like solutions persists long after the evidence proves otherwise. Charter schools cater for about 10 percent of Newark's school-children, and are set up and funded outside of local control:

All Newark's charter schools admit pupils by lottery, so tracking those who applied but didn't get in, as well as those that did, should allow comparisons between equally-motivated children of organised parents, but at different schools. ... Do charter schools' pupils do better at tests because they have been coached intensively at the expense of a broad education? Do charters mean the most motivated students cluster in a few schools, to the detriment of the majority? Do they kick out – or coax out – the toughest to teach? The answers to such questions should soon become clearer. ...That is turning Newark into a magnet for education-policy wonks. (Jun 11, 2009)

Results are not yet available but *The Economist* is waiting in vain. As will be seen in the next chapter, thanks to a range of school lottery admissions schemes, mostly in the US, researchers can already provide some confident answers as to whether charter schools or other forms of semi-commercial educational establishments do better than standard state schools.

School-place lotteries elsewhere

Just to show how widespread the practice is, and how diverse are those who make use of the lottery for school paces, here are some examples from beyond England and the US:

(17) Secondary Schools, New Zealand   2007. This is another example of parental choice. Pupils living in a defined locality of a school or 'home zone' are guaranteed places at their local school. Pupils living outside the 'home zone' can choose places at any school, but ballots (lotteries) are undertaken when the school receives more applications than available places. (Sutton Trust, 2007)

(18) Secondary Schools, Tel-Aviv, Israel 2003. Victor Lavy (2005) reports that until 1994, when students from the five primary schools in poorer districts entered secondary school, for reasons of social mixing they were compelled to attend one of the secondary schools in the northern, more affluent parts of the city. For this they were taken by bus each day. In September 1994 choice of school offered. Each parent/student submitted their preferred school choice in rank order. Then, if demand for places at a particular school was greater than the number available, excess demand is resolved by a lottery.

Public opinion matters: (19) Beijing Eastern City District 1998. Fang Lai (2007) reports that China is implementing on-going education reform. Previously, schools used either a merit-based or geographical proximity-based system for admission to middle schools. Local governments have been replacing this with various forms of random assignment of students to different middle schools. In most cases, the random assignment is to some extent conditional on students' preferred school as shown on their application. In this way the central government hopes to achieve improvement in the equity of educational opportunity while accommodating individual preference of school.

All of this sounds very similar to what is happening in the UK and the US. The usual problems crop up: because middle schools differ widely in performance this has brought about fierce competition between parents for the best schools. The solution is to introduce a lottery for places. What is surprising is the explanation for introducing it. As Fang Lai puts it:

> Introducing such fierce competition and high inequalities in children's access to 'quality schools' at such an early age had been considered both unfair and detrimental to the children's physical and psychological development. Thus, for quite some time, the public demanded an equalization of access to quality schools.

No evidence is produced to show how this public opinion was measured, but it comes as a surprise to discover that it matters so much in a still nominally Communist country.

Because of "the existing dramatic heterogeneity across schools and vested interests" it was claimed that it would be very difficult if not impossible to equalise the resources across schools. So even here it would seem, the authorities have abandoned the (socialist?) hope of making every school a good school. The government had banned merit-based selection because it put unhealthy pressure on the children. As a result, when educational reform was introduced in 1998, it brought about the radical changes in the middle school admission procedure, including the lottery.

The housing market and good schools:
Evidence for house-price effects

It is clear that one of the main motivations for the new English Schools Admissions Code is to prevent the well-off 'buying' places at the best schools. If the mechanism for doing this is school choice by proximity then the prices of houses close to a good school should reflect this. Underlying much of the impetus towards lottery allocation of school places is a belief that parental choice plus lotteries will dilute the house-price premium around good schools and spread it more widely across towns and cities.

The evidence that good schools boost house prices is overwhelming. There have been a number of excellent papers in economic journals reporting such investigations, both in the UK and even more so in the US. I am going to draw on two pairs of authors. The first two, Leech and Campos, are at Warwick University. Professor Dennis Leech is in the Economics Department, but specialises in the effect of voting systems. (Perhaps he might also have something to say about another aspect of lottery use, namely sortition, where a randomly selected group of voters get to decide about matters of public policy.) The other two authors, Steve Gibbons and Stephen Machin, are both in economics departments in London universities. Their on-going interest in the economic impact of education is reflected in several papers on the subject, including our current interest in the effect of good schools on house prices.

Statistical and econometric studies of house prices have long been used to deconstruct and explain the variability in the data. From this it may be possible to filter out what are generally the small effects on overall prices of houses due to a particular attribute. For example the negative effects on the value of properties of dis-amenities like aircraft noise and passing traffic have been studied. The size of positive benefits on the price of a house of environmental improvements and new transport infrastructure have also been estimated. House-price information is widely and cheaply available so provides an ideal test-bed for economists and others to try out their theories. Instead of asking people directly, for example: "How much do you value peace and quiet where you live?", economists *impute* how much value people place on such things. Willingness to pay for some feature reveals, for economists anyway, what that thing is worth. Housing information is also spread geographically, and so creates an opportunity to test the effect of good schools on a neighbourhood.

But is it reliable? Can small differences really be separated out from the huge variability of house prices, not only between different neighbourhoods, different types of housing, but also cope with the surges up and down of the housing market? I have done some research in this area (Boyle, 1984) so I know at first hand the problems and limitations of the technique. This form of analysis requires the use of large amounts of computer power and a suitable statistical package which can perform procedures such as multi-variate regression analysis. This only became practicable from the 1970s onwards with the availability of widespread computing facilities for academics to work with. The papers cited here are very impressive examples of the statistician's art, and have produce some highly accurate and reliable answers. My own benchmark for these analyses is the size of the R-squared coefficients achieved: I managed 79% which was good; these studies got up to 88%. So the answer is: yes, these studies can squeeze the data to reliably reveal the effect of a good school on a neighbourhood.

Gibbons and Machin in their 2007 (G&M07) paper give an excellent summary of the long history of research both in the UK and the US into the effect of school quality on house prices. There is a general consensus amongst researchers that there really is a capitalization of school quality into increased house prices, and that the effect is significant. Based on 11 previous studies G&M state that

> Although we make no attempt at a proper meta-analysis, it is worth noting that the median figure from these studies is about 4% [that is a 4% bonus for school of quality against one which lacks it], with an inter-quartile range of 4%. This stability is remarkable considering the diverse international contexts on which the estimates are based and provides some reassurance that the methods are uncovering a fairly universal figure for the valuation of school quality, at least when standardised in terms of percentage value relative to local housing costs.

Developing their own research on house-prices in London G&M07 produce an estimate of the benefit of having a good school locally, compared that of a not-so-good school. It works out at about £9,000 extra on the value of an average house in London in 2004. Converted to an annualised interest-only benefit suggests that this is worth roughly £450 per year. This looks a reasonable amount when compared with the average per-pupil spend in England's primary schools which was £2750 in the same year. From this G&M07 conclude that a

> ...policy that seeks to break the link between place of residence and school admission seems attractive (such as the lottery systems implemented in some places in the US and proposed recently in some places in England, such as Brighton). Increasing parental choice amongst schools in this way holds the promise of eroding the linkages from school quality to local housing costs.

Note what they are *not* saying: They do not say that lottery-selection *will* banish the house-price premium of a good local school. The lottery may be attractive to policy makers because it suggests it *might* break the link. One assumes that researchers are keenly awaiting the results from Brighton and elsewhere to see if this theory holds up!

In another earlier paper (Gibbons & Machin, 2006; G&M06) the same authors provide a few warnings about this conventional view that good schools boost house prices:

> Admissions constraints [such as the school being full, and requiring some form of limitation on numbers of entrants] have somewhat unexpected effects on the process of school choice...... we conjecture that a school's league-table performance has more of an impact on house prices when schools are over-capacity. Simply because of the over-capacity, admissions-constrained schools attract more attention. In principle, the popularity of a school provides information to prospective home buyers of the quality of schooling they can expect, though in the case of primary phase education in the London area, this information does not seem to have much substantive content.

They also pick up on the possible negative effects of schools, especially when they are not in the top bracket:

> We have also shown that all but the top 1-in-10 schools – judged on their long-run league-table performance – depress prices in their immediate vicinity. Average schools are not desirable local amenities. This may, in part, be explained by 'flight' from the worst schools, but environmental problems also probably contribute. The morning and evening 'school-run' brings traffic and congestion, and there may be additional nuisances such as playground noise that deter buyers.

They also looked at primary schools: G&M06 findings show that a good primary school is a valuable local amenity. This adds some weight to the argument that school admissions procedures at the primary level can lead to selection by income (because richer families can afford better housing). At current prices, parents can expect that if they were to move from an average dwelling outside a weak school to a similar one outside a top over-subscribed school, this would add extra £61,000 or so to the price. That is a premium of 26% on the mean property price in London in 2004. But the effect is very localised: the influence of primary school league-table performance falls quite rapidly with distance, and the effect is halved by about 600m from the school.

The Leech and Campos (2003) study from Coventry (L&C) reports on a study of the effects of a good school on house prices in this industrial city in the English Midlands. Their paper is an excellent example of the diligence which is exercised in order to obtain reliable results uncontaminated by stray or unexplained effects. Their main interest is to overcome the confounding effects such as the obvious feature that good schools are generally in nicer areas. L&C got around this by choosing two schools to compare which were both were in middling areas of the city. The chosen schools were Coundon Court and Alderman Callow.

Coventry did not encourage parental choice. Its admission policy was based on catchment areas, with parents being discouraged from seeking places in popular schools outside these areas. Under these conditions parents in Coventry would have an incentive to move house for the sake of their children's education. This incentive should be reflected in the price of houses.

On the technical side, the study uses a cross sectional sample based on these two schools in Coventry. Differences in housing quality are dealt with by using the technique of hedonic regression and differences in location by sample selection within a block sample design. The sample was chosen from a limited number of locations spanning different catchment areas in order to reduce both observable and unobservable variability while maximising the variation in catchment areas. The results suggest that there are strong school catchment area effects.

L&C tested two indicators of school performance: Quality as indicated by test results, which is reported in published league tables; and Popularity as measured by numbers applying. Coundon Court school had improved its performance; this was reflected in house-price rises in this area. This effect was not observed in the similar Alderman Callow school catchment area, despite both areas featuring middle-ranking houses. Their results show that the better-performing school boosted house prices by about 20 percent (in 2000) compared to the less-well performing one. This suggests a capital value premium of £15-20,000, which would have been the equivalent of an extra £700-£1500 per year on mortgage re-payments.

Comment on house-price and school-effect studies:

It is clear that house prices are positively connected to good local schools, but the Big Question is: will opening up choice, especially lottery-mediated choice, change the house-price premium? Will nice areas with good schools see house-price value drift away to less desirable parts of town? This clearly seems to be the intention of the framers of the English Code on school admissions, and the fear of middle-brow newspaper editors.

It seems galling that the well-off can gain a good education for their children on the cheap by paying extra for a house in the right area. As the statisticians' researches have shown the house-price premium is well below the extra mortgage costs that might be incurred by buying into private education. Why should we allow the financial benefit of a good local school be taken as a private gain? The introduction of school-place lotteries may be one method of clawing back this private gain (or 'rent-capture' in economists' jargon). There could also be other more effective ways of re-capturing this publicly created value, for example by higher local property taxes.

John Adams has written widely[4] about the uncertainties in translating policy into results. One example is the number of lives saved as a result of mandatory seat-belt use for car drivers and passengers. This turned out to be far less than expected or predicted. There are, it seems, always going to be unintended and unanticipated consequences of policy changes. The same will likely happen to the house-price premium for good schools after the introduction of lotteries. There may be some reduction in the good-school bonus, but differences will still remain. Never underestimate the "sharp elbows of the middle classes" when it comes to capturing the best part of publicly provided benefits like schooling.

---

[4] See for example in an article at: *http://hornbeam.cs.ucl.ac.uk/hcs/teaching/ GA10/lec7extra/ carscholeracows.pdf*

Chapter 4

Voucher Lotteries: 'Natural Scientific Experiments'

"Vouchers, it may seem are an idea whose time has come. The proposal to give parents a voucher representing the cost of their children's annual education which can they can 'spend' at the school of their choice (private or state) is not only Tory policy, it is also found favour with New Labour." So says Harry Brighouse (2002), a leading commentator on school-entry policies.

Milwaukee, the Mecca for both US and British voucher advocates is the place to visit for them. In the US vouchers are a highly controversial issue: Google lists five million entries for this topic alone. I will not enter into the controversy here, because my main aim is to look at lotteries not vouchers. But there are some strong insights to be had from the 'natural scientific experiment' when vouchers are allocated by lottery.

The case for vouchers reflects the fundamental belief in free-market economics, most notably espoused by the 'Chicago boys'. Here's what the Chicago Economics Department website says about vouchers:

> Voucher systems would promote free market competition among schools of all types, which would provide schools incentive to improve. Successful schools would attract students, while bad schools would be forced to reform or close. The goal of this system is to localize accountability as opposed to relying on government standards.

This bears a striking resemblance to the case made (in Chapter 1) for parental choice. The difference here is that vouchers with a cash value attached should reinforce the market based incentive. The political agenda is also clear-cut: it is to break the power and control of elected governments both locally and nationally and hand it over to the market. The Chicago economists admit that all may not be well with the voucher idea, and report that

> Typically those against say: That vouchers take funds away from already under-funded public [state-controlled] schools. Private schools aren't subject to as rigorous an oversight; thus, they may not act responsibly, especially when it comes to who gets in: State schools must accept everyone regardless of disabilities, test scores, religion, or other characteristics; private schools can show favouritism or discrimination in selecting students.

There are also objections in the US that vouchers subsidise religion, because they can be used at faith-based schools.

The only satisfactory way to test the theory that vouchers raise academic performance would be to conduct a proper scientific experiment. Randomised experiments are the gold standard of the scientific method. In testing the efficacy of new medical drugs or treatments, regulators require stringent proof that they work. Only a properly conducted experiment, randomised, with double-blind treatments (neither the patient or the doctor doing the treating know which is the real drug, which one is just a dummy 'placebo') will pass muster. Of course it is not deemed ethical to experiment with children's lives, allocating them to different types of school just to test the effects. But when parental choice intervenes, when voucher schemes are in operation, and most crucially when lotteries are used, then the enticing prospect of validated knowledge presents itself. This is what the authors mean by the 'natural scientific experiment'. There are several examples in this chapter which can be interpreted in this way.

Examples of school-place vouchers awarded by lottery

(20) Vouchers for pupils, Columbia, South America 1990s: This description is based on a paper by Angrist and others (2002). For the voucher experiment in Columbia a team of MIT-based economists were involved in the 1990s with a World Bank-funded programme to raise educational standards in developing countries. The chosen method used was to distribute educational vouchers. The authors of this study acknowledge the controversy that rages in the US on the merits of school vouchers, as well as the issue of which system, publicly-funded state education or private fee-paying schooling is more effective. The situation in developing countries, they affirm, is bedevilled by poor-quality state schools, where teachers often do not even turn up to teach. Unlike the US and most other developed countries, in countries like Columbia there is a much larger and thriving private sector which even provides opportunities for poorer families. Of the approximately 3.1 million secondary-school pupils in Colombia in 1995, 37 percent attended private schools: in Bogotá (the capital) this rose to 58 percent.

It was in this context that "one of the largest voucher programs to date", (that is prior to 2002) was implemented, providing 125,000 pupils with vouchers to be used in fee-paying schools. The scheme was launched in November 1991 with advertisements in print and on radio inviting applications in participating cities. To qualify for a voucher, applicants must have been admitted to a participating secondary school (i.e., one that would accept the voucher). The number of vouchers in use in any one year peaked at roughly 90,000 in 1994 and 1995.

The usual conditionality applied to the award of vouchers – only low-income families could apply, children had to have been attending state-run primary schools. The vouchers on offer were hardly generous, worth a mere $190. This was well short of the typical (1998) cost of $340 for private school fees, although the $190 amount was still $24 more than the amount of funding for pupils at state-funded schools. Parents had to top up the shortfall. Not all schools were approved to accept vouchers; those that did generally catered for the less well off.

Allocation of vouchers was devolved down to local cities and towns, which also had to provide some of the funding for the scheme. This degree of local autonomy led to large variations on the numbers of vouchers available in any given area. In some places, all qualified applicants received vouchers; in others where there was an excess of demand for the available supply, a lottery was used to allocate vouchers. "The Bogotá [Head Office] provided software and instructions to regional offices for the purposes of random selection in cases of oversubscription": So there was a conscious attempt to prevent the local mayor fixing 'lottery' vouchers for friends, or maybe even for bribes!

It was this scheme which provided the basis for the 'Randomized Natural Experiment' which could test the hypothesis that private is better than state-funded schooling. Did the use of a lottery to distribute school vouchers amount to a valid scientific experiment? If so it would be a rare event in social science, and is one that holds the promise of validated knowledge.

To check out the experimental credentials the MIT team first had to establish that the characteristics of the lottery winners were similar to that of the losers – that there was no selection bias. Next they tested the effects on educational attainment and other behaviour. Not surprisingly, the voucher winners did significantly better, completing more years of schooling with fewer repeat years than their lottery-losing companions.

Two aspects are worth noting: The team did not rely on school-reported scores on tests. Instead they did follow-up tests of their own on a randomly selected sample of lottery winners and losers. Since the tests were of an internationally standardised type, they could be relied on to give comparable results. Even so the differences in attainment were not huge; 0.2 standard deviations on average. As to the completion and year-repeating rates, the team acknowledge the dubious incentives for private schools: since their funding, including lottery-voucher funding depended on progress, they may have had an extra incentive to push through marginal pupils.

The result: The MIT team concluded that in the particular circumstances of Columbia that vouchers could be a cost-effective method of raising standards. Alas for such 'natural experiments' that is all that can be said; generalisation to other countries or systems does not automatically follow. Nor should the major deficiency in this experiment pass un-noticed: there was no double-blinding. It would be impossible to introduce a 'placebo' treatment in these experiments. Students must have been aware that they were attending a fee-paying school as a result of winning a voucher in a lottery or not. Educationalists are also well aware of 'halo effects' which come from labelling students successes or failures. Winning vouchers by lottery may have had the same effect on some of the pupils involved. Nevertheless, this was a sound attempt to bring some rationality into the debate about vouchers, a scientific test which was only possible because of the need to allocate the vouchers by lottery.

(21) Vouchers for villages, Mexico 1990s: (From Behrman, 2000) This was a full-blown experiment, with formal experimental designs applied to see if a range of social support, including educational vouchers would improve the lot of Mexicans living in the countryside. The scheme was called 'PROGRESA' and included educational vouchers as one of the interventions. A total of 506 villages were identified. Choosing which to assign to the PROGRESA scheme was done randomly. So it was a result of good scientific procedure which led to some villages being lottery winners in this voucher scheme. Formal surveys, structured and semi-structured interviews, focus groups, and workshops were held. This enabled the researchers to ask a series of questions about PROGRESA's effectiveness.

  The result: Educationally, those who received vouchers did better than those who did not. In the dry scientific jargon of the report "The program has a beneficial effect on the educational accumulation process, with statistical tests rejecting the hypothesis that the program had zero effect". This seems to be a very timid attempt to say that the vouchers did some good, but they are not sure how much.

(22) Vouchers, Milwaukee schools 1990 onwards: Despite this being the 'Mecca' for students of voucher schemes (according to

Harry Brighouse) the lottery aspect is somewhat marginal. The Milwaukee Parental Choice Program, which began in the 1990-91 school year, provides an opportunity for students, under specific circumstances, to attend at no charge, private sectarian and non-sectarian schools located in the city of Milwaukee. The scheme appears to award a voucher (worth $6,700 in 2009) to all low-income parents who apply.

Only at the school-entry stage does a lottery come into play. According to Paul Peterson (2002):

..if the demand for voucher places exceeds the supply [at any particular school], a lottery shall be held. In Milwaukee, if many students apply to a particular school for a specific grade, and fewer seats are available, a lottery must be held, except that siblings may be preferred. Private and religious schools can only reject a voucher student through a random lottery. Students cannot be turned away due to their level of academic achievement, disability, religion or the educational background.

The result: There have been a series of studies that exploit the cases where vouchers with lotteries are used – that is for the popular schools. These studies have tried to estimate the educational benefit of effect of attending a private school. I leave it to Cullen, Jacob & Levitt (2003) to summarise the results:

Analyses of this program obtain sharply conflicting estimates of the impact on achievement depending upon the assumptions made to deal with *selective attrition* of lottery losers from the sample.

Although in theory randomization provides an ideal context for the evaluation of school choice, in the Milwaukee case less than half of the unsuccessful applicants returned to the public schools and those who did return were from less educated, lower income families. (Witte 1997). An additional limitation to studies of the Milwaukee program is that direct information on the schools that students applied to is not available, forcing researchers to impute likely application schools (see Rouse 1998 for details).

So contentious is the debate over the merits of voucher schemes that it has even become a text-book study for students. *Chance News* provides source materials for teachers of statistics to enliven their presentations. In a 1996 case-study they reprinted an article from in the Wall Street Journal under the headline '**Dueling professors have Milwaukee dazed over school vouchers'** which lays out the issues. *Chance News* then adds some discussion questions. (See *www.dartmouth.com/chancenews* for details.)

(23) Privately funded vouchers, three US cities 1998: It was reported by *CNN News* (Jun 9, 1998) that billionaire investor Ted Forstmann and friends had created a fund to provide private-school scholarships to students from low-income families. Under the catchy title 'More Dollars for Scholars' it was announced that they will contribute at least $200 million in partial scholarships to help more than 50,000 public school children in selected cities attend private schools. It was said that this looked like an effort to boost the supporters of school choice in the politically charged debate over whether public school students should be able to receive financial help if they choose private schools.

Three programs were established in the Dayton, Ohio metropolitan area, New York City, and Washington, D. C. Researchers were also involved from the beginning in order to test the effectiveness of the program.

> Since scholarships were awarded by means of a lottery in each city, the evaluations of these three programs were all designed as randomized field trials, a research method characteristically used in medical research to determine the effectiveness of drugs or other interventions. When an evaluation takes the form of a randomized field trial, the group receiving the offer of a school voucher is, on average, essentially identical to the control group with which it is compared, the only difference between the two groups being the luck of the lottery draw. Any differences observed during the randomized field trial, therefore, may be attributed to the school the child attended, not to the child's initial ability and family background characteristics, which generally do not differ between the two groups. (Howell & al, 2000)

The voucher programs offered lottery winners annual scholarships of up to $1,700 to help pay tuition at a private elementary school for at least four years. Over 20,000 students filled out initial applications for school vouchers in New York City, over 7,500 applied in Washington, D. C., and over 3,000 applied in Dayton, Ohio. Because the demand exceeded the supply of vouchers available, vouchers in all three cities were awarded by lotteries that gave each family an equal chance of winning a voucher.

Once applications were received, scrutiny began. Applicants attended verification sessions where eligibility was determined, students were given baseline tests, older students filled out short questionnaires, and adult family members completed longer questionnaires. This provided the baseline data; student performances on tests administered at follow-up sessions one and two years after the beginning of the program were also established.

The result: In Howell's study no statistically significant effects on educational attainment, either positive or negative, were observed for students from non-African American ethnic groups who switched from public to private schools with the help of the vouchers. For African American students who were able to switch from public to private schools with voucher support the result was a statistically significant difference. After one year, the improvement averages 0.33 standard deviations, generally thought to be a moderately large effect. Nationwide, differences between black and white test scores are, on average, approximately one standard deviation. The school voucher intervention, after two years, erases, on average, about one-third of that difference. This seems a very meagre result for a great deal of expenditure. A reanalysis of the New York City experiment by Krueger & Zhu (2003), however, suggests that even claims of modest benefits may be overstated.

(24) Universal private school voucher, Sweden 1992 on. By the year 2002, there were over 800 fee-paying primary and secondary schools in Sweden. The universal voucher scheme was introduced in 1992 to widen choice in its school system. The reforms meant that local municipalities became responsible for schools and their financing. Fee-paying schools became eligible to receive funding from municipalities. Pupils could use financial vouchers paid for by municipalities to attend these independent schools. By 2002, these students accounted for about 5 percent of the overall school population. Schools are prohibited from charging fees and are not allowed to select pupils by ability. Students are selected on a first-come-first-served basis. The use of lotteries seems a minor afterthought (Sutton Trust Report, 2007). According to Brighouse (*crookedtimber.org/2004/01/12/*)

> The Swedish voucher scheme has been evaluated positively (and frequently) by Bergstrom and Sandstrom. But it is tiny, and if you read the version of their study put out by the Milton and Rose Friedman Foundation you'll find no evidence of improved scores, and that it is regulated in a way that is unimaginable in the US or UK.

Using the 'Natural Scientific Experiment': Does choice work?

It is thanks to the intrusion of lottery allocation into voucher schemes that this simple question can be put to the test. On the face of it, according to the economists who advocate choice empowered with vouchers it should be no contest. This application of the power of the free market should emerge as a clear-cut winner in raising educational attainment. Here is what Harvard economics professor, and long-time pro-voucher campaigner Mankiw (1999) says:

> If the economic history of the 20th century teaches us anything, it is that an economy based on free and competitive markets serves consumers better than one based on central planning by the government. Schoolchildren, too, should enjoy the benefits of that lesson.

Given that kind of confident assertion it is remarkable that there is still any debate to be had. The introduction of vouchers, if economic theory has any merit, should have quickly produced unequivocally large and sustained improvements in educational attainment. In the case of less-developed countries like Colombia and Mexico vouchers seem to have worked, but the authors are at pains to point out that the local state-funded education they are comparing with is usually pretty dire. The US studies produce more nuanced results, with vouchers and scholarships emerging with, at best, weakly positive results. Milwaukee has produced results which either support or reject the efficacy of voucher schemes in raising school standards, so maybe that example counts as a 'score draw'.

One factor which sets US schooling apart from that in the UK is the strong emphasis on African Americans as a group in need of particular remedial attention. Another is that in the US many of the private (fee-paying) schools that provide the opportunity for voucher-spending are faith-based. Both of these factors should warn us of the difficulties in attempting to generalise the results of particular 'natural experiments' across to different settings, such as those that exist in England and Wales.

But it is to Chicago that I return for what seems to be an assertive answer which would claim to be the last word on vouchers in particular, and school choice in general. The last chapter included the example (13) of the Chicago school board. It operates a parental choice scheme mediated by lottery but does not use vouchers. This scheme was reported by Cullen, Jacob & Levitt (2003). One of the authors, Steven Levitt is a rising star of the economics profession and has become widely known through his book *Freakonomics* (2005). Their paper rejects earlier voucher-based studies as flawed, for example in the Milwaukee case, already quoted, although they acknowledge that non-US examples such as Columbia (20) have shown educational benefit. So what remains of these studies? What can Cullen, Jacob & Levitt offer that is better?

No prizes for guessing that they claim that only their own study of Chicago school students is sufficiently rigorous to settle the issue in the US. Their example (13) has already been described in the previous chapter. It is a simple scheme which allows parents to opt-out of their local school and take a chance in a lottery for entry to what they see is a better one instead. The reasons for parents choosing to do this must surely include achieving higher grades on tests and examinations. Here is what Levitt & Co say about that ambition:

> Surprisingly, we find little evidence that attending sought-after programs provides any benefit on a wide variety of traditional academic measures, including standardized test scores, attendance rates, course-taking, and credit accumulation. This is true despite the fact that those students who win the lotteries attend better high schools along a number of dimensions, including higher peer achievement levels, higher peer graduation rates, and lower levels of poverty.[...]
>
> Our findings present a mixed picture for the potential gains from school choice in urban districts. *If the primary goal is to improve measures of academic achievement and attainment, then it does not appear that this mechanism is effective. The findings are consistent with an even stronger conclusion that attending 'better' schools as measured by a variety of level measures of student performance does not systematically improve short-term academic outcomes.* [my emphasis]
>
> However, open enrollment in the CPS may confer other benefits that are equally worthy, including matching idiosyncratic tastes of parents and students and improving social circumstances.

Emphasis has been added to high-light the most definite and negative conclusion: school choice does not raise academic performance. The confident assertions of the economists are simply wrong.

An opinion piece in *The Times* by Helen Rumbelow (Mar 1, 2007) (the day the Brighton & Hove school lottery hit the national dailies) described the Chicago study like this:

> The results [from the Chicago study] are more than astonishing. They are a kick in the teeth for every one of the 4,000 worried parents who signed a petition against the Brighton lottery; in fact for every parent across the land in a tizz of anxiety as they wait for that imminent

letter from the council telling them which school has been allotted for their little darling.... Having parents who are determined, education-obsessed and aspirational enough to want their child to go to a good school was more important than the school itself. So to every protester in Brighton, I say, relax. The game is rigged. If you are a typical neurotic middle-class nightmare, congratulations. You – and your child – have already won.

Based on the evidence, the conclusion that parental choice does not raise educational attainment now seems to be widely accepted. I have heard John Elliot, Chief Economist at the DfES acknowledged as much at a Conference on (Jun 8, 2006) at Bristol University. At the same venue (on Jun 9, 2009) Helen Ladd, who has studied and written about school-choice in a wide range of countries said: "I believe from the evidence that choice does not lead to higher educational attainment, but does give parental satisfaction."   Further confirmation of the ineffectiveness of parental choice comes from Burges et al. (2009a) "Our reading of the literature is that competition, as it currently exists in England, has not significantly improved the academic performance of schools."

In a rational world this should sound the death-knell for parental choice of schools as well as the market-obsessed vouchers. However it is clear that both parents and politicians are still attracted to the idea, but not for the reasons they express. Parents are choosing for reasons that they well understand. Better schools produce better behaviour, as the evidence shows. Peer group effects may also be beneficial. What cannot be voiced for reasons of political correctness is that middle class parents seek social segregation. Saying that "you get a nicer class of child to mix with at school X" is not the sort of thing school X can put in its prospectus, but that is almost certainly just what parents seem to want. Politicians too, are aware of this, but need to advocate policies like parental choice as the acceptable form of raising educational standards.

Chapter 5

Arguments about School-place Lotteries

In this chapter I look at three different classes of arguments, discussions really, about the use of school-place allocation by lottery. It starts with the most ethereal and finishes with some squalid argumentation. First I report on some heavyweight philosophical wrangling which was sparked off by Brighton & Hove's (by now) notorious decision to 'make education a lottery'. Then I look at the case for 'fair banding' as an alternative to lotteries which is made by the IPPR (Institute for Public Policy Research, a left-leaning think-tank) amongst others. Finally, just to show that the issue has not yet been laid to rest, I present some of the on-going commentary from politicians and the popular press about lotteries-for-education.

Equality of opportunity or equality of outcome:
A philosophical debate

In the previous chapters of this Part I have reported details of the actual use of lotteries for school places. These included the practical case for using lotteries, the experience of using this mechanism and the reaction of the stakeholders who have been involved in the process. The questions which were asked were the practical ones such as: Does it work? Is it better than any alternatives? What do those affected by lottery allocation say they feel about it?

But now it is time to ask the much more difficult questions: is lottery-choosing for school places the right thing to do? is it fair or just? There is a well-established literature on the general philosophical qualities of lottery selection and allocation by Broome, Elster, Goodwin, Stone etc (see references in the Bibliography). Some of these philosophers address questions of the justice of lotteries for education but as one among many of the uses to which lotteries have been put. One useful consequence of Brighton & Hove's decision to use a school-place lottery was that it produced a number of papers which directly address the question: "Is using a lottery to decide school places fair, just or democratic?" I must stress that I am *not* examining the virtues of school choice, or whether there should be selection by schools or if it is right for some parents to buy a better education for their child. The focus here is solely on the rights and wrongs of using a lottery to perform selections, although it sometimes difficult to stick to this narrow brief.

Philosophy condemns school-place lotteries The first shot in the current philosophical argument came from Anthony O'Hear in April 2007. In an editorial in *Philosophy* which is the Journal of the Royal Philosophical Society he roundly condemned the whole idea. This produced some detailed responses (which I had a hand in provoking). The following sections take O'Hear's arguments one by one, and then the response to them. Much of the debate hinges on the twin concepts of equality of opportunity and equality of outcomes.

Argument 1: Life is a lottery   O'Hear quotes a spokeswoman for Brighton Education Committee who suggests that lotteries are by ballot and ballots are fair and democratic. He dismisses this as 'sophistry' (a form of specious or fallacious reasoning) because all of life is a lottery anyway:

> The egalitarian objection to advantages gained by birth, upbringing and character is that one's birth, upbringing and character are lotteries, which we do nothing ourselves to influence or bring about,

and in which for random reasons some gain advantages over others. Even one's ability to work hard at competitions of various sorts is said to derive from dispositions or opportunities one did nothing to merit. So the Brighton – and British – way is henceforth to replace one set of lotteries with another.

In reply to this dismissal of the deliberate use of lotteries for sharing out scarce resources I will draw upon two papers by Peter Stone (with his permission, for which I am most grateful): Stone (2008) "What Can Lotteries Do for Education?" and "Lotteries, Education and Opportunity" (2009):

> —*all forms of selection are arbitrary, so is a lottery:* O'Hear suggests that allocation by social class and allocation by lottery are each morally arbitrary, and therefore there is no ground for preferring one over the other. Clearly, both methods of allocation employ criteria that have no relevance to the allocative problem at hand (in this case, the problem of admitting students to schools). Being a member of a certain class, or drawing a certain number during a random draw, do not provide any reason for being admitted to a school ahead of other students. In that sense, both are 'arbitrary'. But are all non-reasoned methods of allocating goods on a par? If this were the case, then there would be no difference between allocating a kidney transplant on the basis of a fair coin toss and allocating it on the basis of race. This conclusion seems highly dubious. A coin toss, after all, can do things that other non-reasoned procedures cannot. A lottery, by its unpredictable nature, prevents *any* reasons from influencing a role in a decision. It thereby keeps bad or objectionable reasons from playing a role.

Argument 2: Equality of opportunity will not be achieved by a lottery:
Here is what the editorial in *Philosophy* says about this:

> Politicians of all stripes are committed to equality of opportunity. At least almost all of them put it in their statements of fundamental principle. It sounds like something we should all in fairness support, and it is supposed to be free of the radically redistributive and tyrannical implications of attempting to ensure equalities of outcome.

Of course O'Hear is right to question this commitment to the seemingly benign and widely accepted idea of 'equality of opportunity'. It is true that it can be found in the 'mission statements' that adorn the preambles to policy documents. A good example comes from the UK Government: in the Education and Inspections Act 2006 we find that it is intended, among other things, "to promote fair access to educational opportunity". The 2008 Schools Admissions Code gives education authorities a duty to "operate in a fair way that promotes social equity and community cohesion", which surely includes equality of opportunity. I leave aside the purely cynical view that these statements are mere window dressing, pious platitudes of intent. (My favourite guru, W Edwards Deming was renowned for booming out the question: "By what means?" when faced with such vague statements of intent.)

But if the aim of school entry policy is to achieve equality of opportunity then it will not be achieved by a lottery says O'Hear:

> Not that the education lottery will actually achieve equality of opportunity, for some schools will no doubt obstinately prove to be better than others, affording their pupils unequal opportunities in the future. ... [W]ill there be a time when it is simply admitted that equality of opportunity is no more desirable or possible as a political goal than equality of outcome, but simply the same thing under another name?

Stone replies to this:

> — *schools will still vary in quality; students will receive different, unequal outcomes:* Does it really matter that schools remain unequal, and no admissions process – not even a random one – can change that fact? This conclusion does not follow. As noted before, lotteries are unlike other arbitrary processes. Their unpredictability renders it impossible for an agent to act upon the basis of bad or undesirable reasons, at least to the extent that those reasons can only operate in the presence of predictability. This means that lotteries have the ability to block perverse *incentive effects* that other arbitrary processes cannot. Unpredictability need not serve a purely negative role, by rendering certain undesirable forms of action impossible. It can also play a

positive role, by generating incentives for other, more desirable forms of action. For example, the distribution of a good by lot may generate political pressure to mitigate the inequality of the resulting distribution (Calabresi and Bobbitt 1978; Goodwin 2005). Unpredictability means that nobody can ensure the good for themselves, and therefore everyone has an incentive to maximize the number of potential winners (through ample supply of the good) and to ensure that even the losers have it tolerably well (by making up for shortfalls of the good in other ways)

Argument 3: Academic selection is better: O'Hear continues in his editorial to bemoan the demise of the educational system which divided children by ability at the age of 11 based on performance in tests of intelligence:

> It was partly in order to secure equality of opportunity that there has been an assault in Britain on selective education over the past three or four decades, one again supported to a greater or lesser extent by all the major political parties. ... However, three of four decades on, the goal of equality of opportunity remains maddeningly elusive.

O'Hear seems to have overlooked the fact that 'over-subscription' could only happen when parents are free to choose their child's school. Neither selection by an academic entry test nor the somewhat arbitrary criterion of proximity gives parents much choice (apart from defection to the fee-paying sector). As I explained in Chapter 1 it is the parental choice agenda which is the proximate cause of lottery use. If there had been no parental choice then there would be little need for lotteries. Instead he credits the obsession with equality of opportunity as the progenitor of the lottery policy. His criticism would be better directed at economists and others who believe that the 'free market' of parental choice will raise educational standards generally and so achieve the desired result of equally good schools all round.

Argument 4: It's all really about equality of outcome (not opportunity): O'Hear's claims that "if the goal really is to make schools more equal, then isn't what's at stake here really equality of outcome, not equality of opportunity? and equality of opportunity degenerates into an attempt at equality of outcomes which is absurd":

Stone replies to this at some length:

In fact, I would concede the point – whatever else lotteries can accomplish when employed to admit students to desirable schools, they do not provide equality of opportunity, at least to the extent that equality of opportunity is distinct from equality of outcome. This conclusion, however, has little normative bite unless two further implications are drawn from it, implications that O'Hear endorses. First, equality of opportunity and equality of outcome are identical. Second, the case for equality of opportunity in education and the case for equality of outcome in education are identical, and both are undesirable. Neither implication, however, follows from O'Hear's valid effort to separate the case for lotteries from equality of opportunity as a distinct value. I shall conclude this section by elaborating upon this denial.

The claim that equality of opportunity is equivalent to equality of outcome depends upon a very specific understanding of the former concept. On this understanding, an individual's relative success in competing for goods (university admissions, desirable jobs, etc.) ought not to depend upon morally arbitrary facts. If one individual obtains such a good, and another does not, then the reason for this difference cannot be any morally arbitrary difference between the two. Traditionally, this is interpreted to mean any facts that are outside the control of the individuals in question. Differences in attainment should reflect differences of choice on the part of the individuals, and nothing else. But arguably everything an individual does is the result of features of his situation that are outside his control. Even the choices he makes depend upon his ability to exert effort, and this ability may arguably the product of his genes, upbringing, and education, all of which were outside his control (Rawls 1999, p. 89). The logic of this argument thus leads to the conclusion that *all* differences between individuals are arbitrary, and thus every individual ought to receive exactly the same thing. Thus, equality of opportunity transforms, in a seemingly inexorable manner, to equality of outcome.

But this inexorability is more apparent than real. For these are other ways of understanding the concept of equality of opportunity. Lesley Jacobs, for example, contrasts the above conception with a conception of equality of opportunity as depending upon a *'level playing field.'* "The main idea here," Jacobs continues, "is that equality of opportunity requires everyone to enter competitions [for goods] at roughly the same starting position" (Jacob's emphasis; Jacobs 2003, p. 14). This approach permits some factors to enter into the success individuals have in competing for goods (natural talent, effort), while excluding others (race, religion, economic background). This conception permits people to receive unequal amounts of various goods on the basis of relevant factors, even if those factors are arbitrary in the sense of being outside anyone's control. For this reason, it eludes the reduction of equality of opportunity to equality of outcome that concerns O'Hear.

If equality of opportunity is distinct from equality of outcome, at least upon some understandings of the former concept, then which (if any) is desirable in the case of school admissions? I would argue that at the primary and secondary school levels, it is equality of outcome, not equality of opportunity, that is the relevant value (although not necessarily the only value). There are two reasons for this. First, the agents involved are not the type of agents to whom equality of opportunity can generally apply. Second, the good in question is not the type of good for which equality of opportunity is an appropriate principle of allocation.

If one were to speak of equality of opportunity as the governing value regarding school admission processes, then one would be committed to a view in which the individuals taking part in these processes — underage children — were engaged in a competition for the good of education. This view is flawed in two respects. First, children lack the moral and intellectual standing to engage in such competition, at least when anything substantive is at stake. They lack the capacities to make binding decisions for which they can be held morally or legally accountable, at least to the same extent as adults. This is why they cannot sign legally binding contracts, and why they are normally not punished as severely as adults for crimes they may commit. For this reason, it seems particularly perverse to suggest that one first-grader should be able to get into his most desired school, while another cannot, because the first tried harder, or sacrificed more, than the second. And these are all ideas associated with equality of opportunity. Put another way, the distinctions we readily make between adults when they compete for goods—distinctions between those who try hard and those who slack off, between the talented and the slow-witted—seem inappropriate as reasons for favoring some underage children over others, at least when the stakes are at all significant. And this leaves no real basis for distinguishing between them; it leaves little as a goal, in other words, except equality of outcome.

Second, there are some goods that are not meant to be distributed through competition. It once again seems perverse, for example, to suggest that sick people should "compete" for access to cures for their ailments (even though this competition is all-too real in a market-driven health industry). Primary and secondary education is similarly unsuited for competitive distribution. The primary, though not the only, purpose behind education at this level is to ensure that all citizens have the basic skills necessary to be functioning members of society. But upon this understanding, it would make no sense for society to have children compete for the chance to obtain these skills; instead, society should ensure that all citizens develop them. [Stone quotes the example of teaching children to read where equality of outcome is desired.]

Successful primary and secondary schooling, to a very large extent, is the sort of good that everyone should receive equally. That seems to follow from the nature of the good in question. When a good is to be distributed among children, there is a *prima facie* case for distributing it equally. When the good of primary and secondary education—which centrally involves the transfer of basic skills—is to be distributed, there is also a *prima facie* case for distributing it equally. When the good of primary and secondary education is to be distributed among children (as it usually is), the case for distributing it equally thus becomes extremely strong. But should this fact concern anyone, given the disrepute into which equality of outcome as an ideal has fallen in recent times? Not if my description of the good at stake is adequate. There is little danger in a Stalinist insistence on conformity emerging out of a commitment to teach all small children how to read. To insist otherwise is to insist that the meritocratic logic of competition must apply in all areas of human life. And the dangers posed by such an insistence are just as real as the dangers posed by a misplaced devotion to equality of outcome.

So if this form of 'equality of opportunity' is both valid and desirable, what part could the use of lotteries play? Stone continues:

> The lottery provides a way out to allocative authorities faced with this dilemma that is consistent with equality of treatment. Students (with equally valid claims to schooling) are treated equally, obviously, when they are sent to equally good schools. But where this proves impossible, because schools remain unequal, students are still treated equally when a lottery is used to decide which of them win admission to the best schools. They are treated equally because, despite the unequal outcomes, they are still being treated *impartially*. In employing random selection, admission authorities do not favor some students over others for any (presumably illegitimate) reasons; rather, they favored some over others for no reason whatsoever. They cannot help but will that some students gain admission to good schools while other, equally worthy students do not. But they can avoid willing that any *particular* set of students gain admission to good schools while the others do not. And this is all that can be demanded, in terms of equality of treatment, in the face of persistently unequal schools.

Note that lotteries, because of their unpredictable nature, can ensure equality of treatment in ways that other arbitrary procedures cannot. If school admission authorities admitted students on the basis of socioeconomic status, then they would clearly be distinguishing between students on an inadmissible basis. They would be using an indefensible reason for favoring some students over others. But a lottery keeps out all reasons for favoring some students over others — and this is good, because all reasons are inadmissible reasons in this case. This provides further support to

> my earlier claim that not all 'arbitrary' methods of distinguishing
> between people are alike.

I will leave readers to decide where they stand, philosophically, on the ideas of equality of opportunity and equality of outcome, especially in relation to the use of lotteries to distribute school places when demand exceeds supply. These debates are important in clarifying the issues. I am most grateful to Peter Stone for allowing me to reproduce this extended and lucid extract from his papers.

In another response to O'Hear's editorial Saunders (2008) takes a more technical view based on the Contractualism ideas of Scanlon, Harsanyi and probably the best-known of all Rawls. Saunders contrasts possible methods of distribution of the prize of a school-place: this could be by selection (tests), auction (selling the place to the highest bidder) or using a lottery. Since selection and auction are ruled out for reasons which are well-known, then the use of lotteries is the remaining option.

> ..both Rawls and Scanlon offer contractualist theories that make lotteries a requirement of justice in given cases. In Scanlon's case, this is fairly obvious, for those with equal claims to a good can reasonably reject any procedure that gives them less than equal chances. In Rawl's case the appeal to the original position may lead one to assume that it is unnecessary to implement an artificial lottery, as arbitrary natural characteristics can be appealed to instead. I have argued, however that 'natural lotteries' are only just where outcomes do not depend on identifying characteristics of individuals,...

There are many more avenues that might be explored concerning equality of opportunity when considering the use of lotteries. They may help administrators and parents decide, but in themselves do not make the case for or against school-place lotteries.

An alternative to lotteries: 'fair banding'

Banding has emerged from several of the examples so far as a significant alternative or even supplementary method of allocating school places. For example Haberdashers' Aske's (4) has abandoned its lottery scheme in favour of banding plus proximity, where applicants are given an academic test and then put in different bands according to ability. Those who live closest to the school in each band are then offered a place. Another form of banding might be to take a quota for pupils eligible for free school lunches, or it might involve racial groups, with a quota of pupils selected from each group. This is one way to force schools to take in a social mix which reflects their population.

This case for 'fair banding' is elaborated in an IPPR paper by Tough & Brooks (2007), which identifies the key issue preventing choice from doing its intended job: that just because parents have choice does not mean that they will use it:

> We should also be concerned about the distinction between the formal existence of choice and whether it is equally utilised by all parents. Segregation by ability and social class in schools is due in part to which parents apply to which schools. The mechanism of choice to drive standards is premised on the idea that parents will make 'rational' decisions about which school to apply to based on school performance.

Helen Jarvis writing in *The Guardian* (Mar 1, 2007) has even tried to link this with the introduction of school-place lotteries by suggesting that the **Poor hindered by school lotteries**. That was the headline, but the story had little to do with lotteries. This was based entirely on the perceived ineptitude of working-class parents in working their way through the system, no matter how simple it was made. Based on her own study (Jarvis, 2008) she said:

> Our research suggests that lotteries of oversubscribed school places would produce the worst of both worlds – greater educational polarisation and longer, more environmentally damaging car journeys to distant schools by middle-class parents. It is interesting that in Brighton, a Labour-controlled authority is proposing such a

system on the grounds of fairness and equality of opportunity, whilst our research suggests it may have exactly the opposite result.

It cannot be denied that choice-plus-lotteries will result in more children travelling further distances. But what of the other charge: because of the ineptitude of working class parents there will inevitably be a polarization, with schools becoming more socially segregated?

At the heart of this debate is the "sharp elbows of the middle classes"; that some parents are simply more determined to make the effort to secure better places for their children. This is supported by the evidence (again from Tough & Brooks 2007):

> Families where the mother has a degree are twice as likely to apply to a school outside their local authority as families where the mother has no qualifications, and parents from lower socio-economic backgrounds are more likely to consider their child's friendship groups and proximity to the school as more important than its performance table position. On the other hand, academic factors are more likely to be relevant in establishing which schools to apply to for mothers in a non-manual social class. There are also differences between factors used by different ethnic groups as well as social classes. For example, black parents consider discipline and resource levels to be more important than other groups do. Some parents are also better equipped to work the system to make sure they get what they want. Mothers with a degree or higher qualification are three times more likely to say they know how popular schools allocate places .

It is clear from these comments that the groups that UK politicians most want to help – parents of children from less well-off backgrounds – simply cannot be trusted to make the effort to use a system which allows parental choice. Whether the element of lottery is added onto that choice seems immaterial. The crafty middle-classes in cahoots with the better schools will, it seems, always find ways of bending the system, even a lottery-based one, to their advantage. To thwart their anticipated machinations, even when a lottery is used, further safeguards have been proposed:

Parental Help: Information and assertiveness: The School Admission Code calls for choice advisors to be present in every school to assist parents. Schools too, should be required to be open with information about their schools. This idea is supported by Tough and Brooks.

Monitoring of Outcomes: Rather than accept that lotteries will produce the socially desired results Tough & Brooks insist that it is better to be pro-active; that it is

> ...better to 'monitor and decide'. We do not need to inspect local admissions arrangements to determine whether they are working in a way that is likely to lead to fair outcomes. We can simply measure the results of the process, and in particular we can measure how the degree of segregation by prior attainment, social class and ethnicity in schools changes as a result of the introduction of the new measures. If there is no improvement then we have a good reason to believe that the changes are insufficient and that we should go further.

The reasons why monitoring is essential are that

> ...regardless of the rules of the admissions system, it will always be in a school's interests to try to select the most able pupils if it can do so. While many schools act responsibly, we present evidence that some schools are covertly selecting their pupils, and that these are much more likely to be schools who have authority over their own admissions.

Centralized control over admissions: Tough & Brooks produce evidence of cheating behaviour by schools in admissions procedures: (p16)

> ... schools who are their own admission authorities do have more potentially selective admissions criteria than those schools whose admissions are set by the local authority. In addition, analysis of who goes to which schools corroborates the hypothesis that autonomous schools are covertly selecting pupils in terms of ability and socio-economic status. The capability of schools to administer their own admissions appears to be key to this process.

They conclude that no school should administer its own admissions or be its own admissions authority.

In calling for choice advisors, monitoring and central admissions, Tough & Brooks have clearly picked up on the ideas of the Theory of Public Choice. They assume, and with some evidence, that schools will twist the system for their own benefit, by choosing brighter, nicer children. The middle class parents too, will (not unreasonably) connive with this in seeking to get their children into better schools. These pressures exist, but the authors presume that choice-plus-lottery will do little to attenuate them. So despairing are they of any improvement wrought by a simple lottery-based system that they feel it is necessary to impose significant extra bureaucratic burdens on schools and the education authorities. Requiring all students to produce information about their ethnicity and socio-economic status is not only burdensome, but might be considered an intrusion on individuals' privacy too.

There is a counter-argument, which is that choice-plus-lottery does away with the need for such clumsy, intrusive monitoring. If, as was found in Charlotte-Mecklenburg (15), parents *choose* to re-segregate their schools, if working-class parents *prefer* to send their children to the local school, why should egalitarians object? The benefits to society of social and ethnic mixing need to be spelt out clearly before over-riding the wishes of parents.

How does 'fair banding' compare with lottery selection? Tough & Brooks conclude that,

> 'Fair banding' is generally taken to mean selecting an intake so that its spread of ability is representative of a wider population. This wider population could be all the applicants to a particular school or group of schools, or the whole pupil population in a geographical area such as a local authority or nationally, and these two options have very different implications.

> Fair banding actually has very similar effects to the random allocation of pupils, for example by lottery, as any random sample of sufficient size is likely to reflect the characteristics of its population.

An alternative to fair banding would thus be to hold a lottery to allocate places to over-subscribed schools. As with banding, lotteries can be combined with other criteria, for example catchment areas, within which oversubscribed schools could run lotteries to allocate places. Lotteries have the key advantage that they can break up tight socio-economic/geographical monopolies around popular schools that use proximity as their current over-subscription criteria. Lotteries may thus be a step in the right direction in some cases.

However, they achieve the objective of a fairer distribution of ability across the schools system in a somewhat opaque way. We think it is better from a procedural fairness perspective to argue openly for a fair distribution of ability. In addition, while from a technical point of view the random allocations determined by lotteries can be considered fair, they may not be perceived to be so by the public because they lack apparent rationale. *We therefore prefer the use of fair banding by ability to the use of random lotteries.*

Lotteries to decide school places?
Low politics and the popular press

Later experience with the School Admission Code shows that there is still uneasiness about the use of lotteries: By 2009, Ed Balls, who is the Children, Schools and Families (i.e. Education) Minister seemed to be wavering in his support for the use of lotteries when he was reported (by *Reuters* Mar 2, 2009) as saying:

"I know the issue of lotteries is causing some concern to parents around the country. I have sympathy with the view that a lottery system can feel arbitrary, random and hard to explain to children in Years 5 and 6 who don't know what's going to happen and don't know which children in their class they're going to going on to secondary school with." Ed Balls has said that he had asked the Chief Schools Adjudicator to review the use and fairness of school admission ballots.

The downmarket *Sun* newspaper's take on this story was in no doubt about the outcome of the Adjudicator's review (Mar 2, 2009):

> **School selection ballot gets axe:** The lottery system for allocating school places is set to be dumped, it emerged yesterday. Children's Secretary Ed Balls has admitted the random selection ballots can be "pretty unfair". Currently around 25 local authorities pull names out of a hat to decide which kids go to popular state schools. Mr Balls called situations where twins are put in different schools and local kids are refused places "ridiculous".

The behaviour of Ed Balls, the Education Minister looks like a typical politician's move: when something crops up which looks unpopular or might affect swing voters, say you are against it and demand an Enquiry. Judging by the Adjudicators' previous pronouncements, this enquiry will have only one result, despite what the Sun newspaper might claim. Following some mature reflection, the use of the lottery will be endorsed. (I will be considering these practical aspects of political processes in more detail at the end of Chapter 8.)

The Adjudicator worked quickly. As part of the annual review process, her office queried all the Local Authorities (LAs) in England. The Adjudicator's Report *On the use of random allocation in admission arrangements for schools in England* was published in September 2009. The Secretary of State wished to know

1. how widely random allocation was being used or proposed.
2. whether it produced fair outcomes for children and parents.
3. what was the evidence of parental reaction and understanding of the system.

Q1. How widely is lottery used? Only three LAs indicated that they made significant use of a lottery for the main allocation of places. These were Brighton & Hove (11), Hertfordshire (12) and Northamptonshire. I have already included details of the lottery schemes for Brighton & Hove as well as Hertfordshire in Chapter 3 based on this report. The Adjudicator was unclear whether Northamptonshire really was using a lottery.

Of the remaining 150 LAs that responded, about 20 per cent stated that that lotteries are only used as tie-breakers. The reasons why ties might arise included: the case of twins or multiple births; with equidistant applicants; to distinguish between applicants in blocks of flats; for the last place when the infant class size limit would be breached; in selective schools where applicants have equal test scores. These are not factors which would affect many applicants, nor would the use of lottery be contentious in these cases.

Q2. Does it produce fair outcomes for parents and students? Comments from the three main users of the lottery system as was seen earlier (in examples 11 and 12) were generally positive. Northamptonshire's comments on fairness related to one single sex girl's school only. They believe the system to be fair as it enables parents from across Northamptonshire a chance of being allocated a place at the only single sex girls school in the town.

A number of the LAs which did *not* use random allocation in any significant way felt it necessary to add their own comment on the *un*-fairness of using lotteries. All were opposed to random allocation and none were considering its introduction. Typical comments were as follows:

– Use as a tie-break is fine but anything more general counteracts valued aims of prioritising local residents over more distant ones, raises sustainability of transport issues and calls into question the transparency of arrangements. The prospectus provides parents with information to assess their prospects of success when applying to particular schools. This cannot be done if random allocation is used;
– Concern that it would be difficult to defend with appeals panels;
– Would not work in a rural LA where towns tend to be served by one secondary school;
– Would create uncertainty for parents who still look to their local school;
– At odds with principle of local schools for local children;
– Could potentially have a major impact on transport policy, costs and the thrust towards sustainable travel to school;

– Few LAs will adopt because of its high negative profile in the media (a particular reference to the media focus earlier this year).

Remember, all these comments are from those LAs which are *not* using random allocation. Perhaps they should visit one of the three LA areas which do, and find out what is really going on!

Q3. What is the parental reaction to and understanding of the system? The Adjudicator did not find it possible to undertake a proper survey of parents within areas using random allocation to determine their reactions at first-hand. Instead she relied on comments from the LAs. We have already seen the reaction from Brighton & Hove where "overall, parents have accepted the change in a relatively short time." Herefordshire noted that "the introduction of the random element has reduced the predictability of allocation outcomes," although no significant level of concern has been officially raised or noted.

Northamptonshire LA commented that "parents find the joint use of equal preference and random allocation confusing. Some are angry that their child's education rests on a randomizer, but once the current and previous systems are explained to them, they are said to '*understand*'". (It is not clear whether this means they are any less angry).

The Adjudicator added that from their own experience "objections to their Office from parents which mention elements of random allocation have been very few".

Overall the Adjudicator concluded that

> There seems little appetite to introduce random allocation amongst LAs not currently using it any real sense (i.e. the majority). They are concerned that it would act against the principle of local schools for local children, be inconsistent with the Government's green agenda in that it cannot be said to promote sustainable travel to school and that it would make it more difficult for parents to judge the likelihood of success when applying for school places.

Judging by the comments which came from the three LAs which were satisfied with their use of lotteries it was suggested that other LAs should consider using them too:

The findings of this exercise suggest that there is sufficient scope for LAs and other admission authorities to use random allocation if they, and their communities, believe it would be useful in their circumstances.

And with that came the final **Recommendation:** that the current legislation and guidance in the Code is appropriate, and does not currently need to change. Ed Balls the Education Minister replied (on the Departmental website *www.dcsf.gov.uk*): "I am reassured by your evidence that the use of random allocation provides a valid contribution to fair access to school places, and by your conclusion that the current legislation and guidance is appropriate."

Conclusion The case for randomly allocating school places has been tried in England and has passed with flying colours. The use of lotteries is sound and is workable. Parents have come to accept the value of this method of selection. Let's hope that this lesson is remembered in the future.

Part II:
Lotteries with
Academic Selection

Chapter 6

Schools Selecting Academically: Measuring Ability

Selection for school entry by an academic test and the use of lotteries might seem to be mutually exclusive, yet in this chapter I will make the connection. There are a few examples where school entry uses the combination of academic selection and lotteries. But first I would like to review the troubled yet highly successful history of tests of intelligence.

Academic selection on the basis of ability:

Since schools and colleges are primarily academic institutions it seems obvious that they should choose entrants on grounds of academic ability. Many schools have made, and are still making use of some form of academic entry test. One example of these tests is the Common Entrance examination used by British public (fee-paying) schools. For university entrance, the widespread use of SATs in the US will be considered later. SATs are a form of IQ test which aims to measure the innate ability of applicants. But the academic test which looms largest in the British, or more specifically the English and Welsh consciousness is the '11-plus'.

In an effort to establish a more rational basis for selecting and rejecting candidates, and in particular identifying hidden talent, tests of intelligence were developed, starting over 100 years ago, most notably by Spearman. These tests have been in widespread use ever since. The Stanford-Binet test of IQ

(Intelligence Quotient) has been widely used, and correlates well with human abilities.

Discriminating between people on the basis of an IQ test may have had a troubled history. Revelations that Sir Cyril Burt, one of the pioneers of testing, may have faked much of his data on monozygotic twin studies (Taylor, 1980) casts a shadow over such endeavours. More controversial is the questionable use of IQ statistics to support racist views. One unpleasant example of this is the best-selling book by Herrnstein and Murray on the *Bell Curve* (1994). It might seem foolhardy to venture into such controversial territory, but I do so for a good reason: the testing of IQ to predict short run academic performance has been intensively studied, and there is a wealth of experience to draw upon. This section draws heavily on Vernon (1957) who reviewed the evidence for the effectiveness of the 11-plus IQ test. Later on Gipps and Murphy (1994) covered some of the same ground but did not challenge any of the earlier figures which were produced concerning the accuracy and reliability of this test.

The measure of success for the 11-plus test was very simple: how well did the test predict the performance of the cohort five years later at the General Certificate of Education (national, public) examinations? The short answer is very well indeed, especially compared with alternative methods of selection and prediction. The alternative selection methods which were used included standardized tests in mathematics and English, ranking by teachers and special entrance examinations set by individual schools. A global figure for the reliability of IQ tests in predicting later examination scores was estimated by Vernon at a correlation coefficient of 0.70. All other methods of testing showed lower correlations.

All of this seems to point towards IQ testing as the nearest thing to an ideal form of selection for academic ability. If achievement in examinations is the criterion for success in schooling then this is by far the best means to procure it. The 11-plus still has its advocates, especially amongst those from humble backgrounds who feel that it gave them their best chance in life.

How the 11-plus was implemented: The objective of the British 11-plus test was to measure the IQ of all children in the 11-year-old cohort within each local education authority (LEA). This could involve tens of thousands of school-children in a single authority (borough), so there was plenty of scope to establish fair and efficient procedures. On the basis of their scores on the test, a percentage of the pupils from the cohort, which ranged from 14 percent in Nottinghamshire to 60 percent in Merionethshire[5], were allocated to Grammar schools, in the belief that they could benefit from an academic style of education. This was a straight-forward quota selection system. A cut-off score had to be calculated; those who fell below were deemed to have 'failed', those above 'passed' and went on to Grammar school. 'Pass' and 'fail' are in quotes because this was portrayed, not as a competition, but as a sorting process which found the school best suited to a child's talents. Parents and pupils had no such illusions. (There may have been a small amount of discretion for borderline candidates, which I will look at later in this chapter).

Kline (1991), who is a notable critic of the use of IQ tests, admits that "the application of psychometrics [IQ testing] is one of the few technological successes in psychology". He concludes that "If we take the correlation between intelligence and academic success across a whole range of ability it is likely to be substantial, around 0.5" – that 50% of ability and achievement can be explained by the score on an IQ test[6]. So IQ tests and their close cousin the US SATs tests are valid, quite probably the best, and maybe the only way of identifying those with potential to succeed.

The Economist (Mar 12, 2005) makes a spirited defence of SATs: "If universities admitted students purely on the basis of their

---

[5] you will search in vain for Merionethshire on today's maps of Wales. It was mostly subsumed into the new county of Gwynedd during local government re-organisation. In common with the rest of Wales it no longer uses the 11-plus exams.

[6] Sharp-eyed readers may have spotted the discrepancy between the 0.5 figure here and the 0.7 value quoted earlier. Those with a statistical training will realise that 0.7 squared is 0.5; one is the correlation coefficient, the other is the index of determination, so are essentially the same measure.

grades and test scores, as they should, the proportion of successful poor students would actually go up rather than down." The alternatives which the Economist was criticising were entry systems which used additional tests, or worst of all interviews. These will be examined more closely in the next chapter.

Examples where a lottery is used in academic selection:

So if IQ tests are to be used, mainly because they are so effective, how could they be combined with a lottery? In its simplest form all those scoring above a predetermined score would be accepted; if there were more high scorers than places then a lottery would decide the winners. Such schemes exist and are generally known as a 'threshold lotteries'.

Although academic selection for some schools still persists in some areas of England, I have found no example where it is combined with a lottery. In the US, academic selection for high school entry is unusual, but where it exists has produced some rare examples of threshold lotteries. These are the 'magnet schools' which are another version of Charter schools or Academies, which aim to break out of the one-size-fits-all 'bog standard Comprehensive' to use the well-worn phrase.

(25) Magnet Schools, Tennessee 2009: According to the Metropolitan Nashville Public School's website (*www.mnps.org*) there are three magnet schools in Davidson County which have academic entry requirements. Students are selected by lottery from those who meet the enrolment requirements. These are based on prior academic performance, which is expressed thus:

> The **enrollment requirements** are 85 or above average for the spring semester of last year and the 1st grade period of the current school year with no failing grades, **and** current Metro students must have achievement test (CRT) scores ADVANCED in both math and reading, and non Metro students must have reading and math stanine scores on a norm-referenced achievement test equaling 14 or above (no rounding).

I'm sure that is crystal-clear to local applicants, or at least their advisors and counsellors!

(26) Central Magnet School, Bridgeport, Connecticut 2005: Bridgeport runs three elementary magnet schools, open to all, which also make use of a lottery to decide entrants. There is just one single magnet school – Central High School – which in 2005 adopted an academic hurdle for applicants and then selected by lottery. To qualify for acceptance in the lottery students had to have obtained C+ grades in all subjects. The website then explains the selection process as:

> The lottery places the qualified applicants in numbered positions on a wait list for entry. Admittance to Central Magnet is determined by the number of available seats and the next position of qualified applicants on the wait list. The wait list is maintained for eighteen months. (from *www.bridgeportedu.com*)

Currently (2009) no mention is made of the use of a lottery, so perhaps supply and demand for places has balanced out.

Lowell High Magnet School, San Francisco 1995, 2002: A threshold lotteries that did *not* happen: Both of the previous examples are fairly low-key, and do not seem to have caused any dispute. For another academically selective school, Lowell High Magnet School in San Francisco, the suggestion that it *might* adopt a threshold lottery sparked off a vigorous debate. Lowell is the oldest high school in the western states of the U.S., and maintains a high reputation for academic excellence. It has been involved in some controversies over the racial composition of its intake, including one case in the 1990's brought by Chinese-American citizens objecting to race-based admissions policies. As a result race was no longer used to select students; instead socio-economic factors were taken into account for a small number of places (seats) (*Wikipedia on Lowell*). The main method of selection was to be an academic test with a cut-off score which was the same regardless of ethnic classification. The result is that the student body of Lowell has a preponderance of 'East Asian' students.

Grofman & Merrill (2004) state that the use of a threshold lottery selection scheme was specifically suggested by Guinier (2002). In this way Lowell School's problem of an excess of ethnic Chinese students could be overcome, and its racially-determined quota system, with higher scores for ethnic Chinese students could be eliminated. This idea was not adopted; no mention is made of any form of lottery for Lowell in 2009.

Lowell also figured in an earlier comment by Matloff (1995):

..affirmative action has seen some abominable implementations. For instance, the (court-ordered) admissions policy for San Francisco's prestigious Lowell High School is so overtly race-conscious that it even invents its own 'races,' setting criteria for Chinese American applicants that are different from those for other Asian American applicants.

He goes on to suggest that instead of race-norming the answer is:

some threshold values should be established for numerics such as SAT scores, below which there is little expectation of success at this school. But, after having set such threshold values, there is, except for very special cases, really no defensible reason for further comparison of test scores among applicants. Once the applicant pool has been narrowed in this manner, a sensible policy would be that school admissions officers use a lottery for selecting applicants. At most schools, this would produce the desired diversity in race and gender that affirmative action advocates consider so important. But at the same time such a procedure would be simple, fair and race/gender-blind, which would go a long way toward answering affirmative action's critics.

The claim is that a 'threshold lottery' would produce a representative intake for an unusual school like Lowell, but does this claim stand up?

In their paper Grofman & Merrill (2004) provide considerable background material on the measurement of IQ and how it differs between racial groups as well as by gender. In order to test the efficacy of threshold lotteries as an alternative to affirmative action they analysed the likely outcome of threshold-with-lottery entry schemes for academically selective schools. Their technique was mathematical, and involved simulating distributions which differed between groups. This could be where the groups showed different mean scores, but with identical variances; alternatively the mean scores of the groups could be the same, but the variance (spread) different. These characteristics have been found in populations which have been investigated by earlier researchers when investigating variations in SAT scores.

The purpose of Grofman & Merill's analysis was to compare the proposed threshold lottery admission system for schools with two alternatives: a pure highest-test-score always wins, and; affirmative action which requires a quota of the highest scoring applicants from each group. The authors explore a wide range of different scenarios using the same mathematical logic and provide useful material to compare higher or lower thresholds. They point to the somewhat obvious conclusion that although lower thresholds produce a more representative mix, the expected academic performance of the group would suffer. They conclude:

> Our SAT example shows that when groups differ significantly in test scores, such lottery rules may not yield results that are particularly close to proportionality unless the threshold for acceptance is set unreasonably low.

This result is hardly surprising, nor would it require complicated mathematics to work out that threshold lotteries will not yield a result that gives every group, whatever its mean score, places in proportion to their numbers. But the result would be at the very least more representative than a pure highest-score-always-wins.

In a similar exercise Carnevale & Rose (2003) carried out the same sort of algebraic analysis based on the evidence provided by SAT scores and applied it to university entrants. They posit four criteria for the acceptability of threshold lotteries for admissions.

– *Would it meet with Public Approval:* Following a purpose-built survey they found that "fully 83 percent of the public disagree with the idea that colleges and universities should use a lottery to choose which students are admitted". Since this is a hypothetical question (no university actually uses a simple lottery for admissions), and with the public's well-known aversion to random selection (see surveys in Chapter 2) this result is much as might be expected. However the authors interpret this result as an indication of "our cultural bias in favor of individuals over groups and a strong preference for merit-based opportunity".

– *Would it produce the desired Racial and Ethnic Diversity.* Using a similar mathematical modelling approach used by Grofman & Merill they conclude that a threshold lottery would not increase the share of minorities in the qualified pool over current levels. But they add that "The low shares of minorities in the qualified pool reflect the fact that Blacks and Hispanics are much less likely than Whites to take the SAT or ACT or to score above 900" (the threshold score they used for this exercise).

– *Would it increase the Socioeconomic Diversity of the intake?* "Socioeconomic diversity would increase substantially using a lottery to create the qualified pool with only 45 percent coming from the top SES quartile and 27 percent from the bottom two SES quartiles".

– *Would it affect the final college performance of the group selected by lottery?* The likely result would be "dramatically reduced graduation rates or lowered standards in selective colleges". How 'dramatic' or 'lowered' is not spelled out by the authors. This deficiency will be made good when I examine the scheme used in the Netherlands for medical school entrants. There the results are indeed lower, but not dramatically so!

There are two difficulties with this study: one is that it has been undertaken by the commercial organisation which provides the material on which SATs are implemented. The second difficulty is that in criticising threshold-lotteries for university entrance they are shooting at a straw man: although some commentators (Astin, Guinier, Karabel) have suggested threshold lotteries for university entrance, nowhere have schemes like this been implemented. Also school entrance at the age of 11 or 12 and admission to a university at 18 or later present different selection problems.

Zwick (2007) goes further, using these papers to reject all forms of lotteries:

But random selection does not automatically imply fairness. The decision to treat all individuals – or individuals 'above a threshold' – as interchangeable requires justification, just as any other selection principle does. And dissatisfaction with the status quo is not an adequate justification. We as a society need to do the hard work of crafting admissions policies that are consistent with our ethical and educational principles. We can do better than casting lots.

This seems to be based on wishful thinking, and an over-interpretation. Just saying that threshold lotteries are not as efficacious as affirmative action does not mean that all forms of lottery choosing are inadequate. While mathematical models may produce results which seem to confirm the prejudices of the authors, there is little substitute for practical experience.

Left out of such abstract modelling are possible dynamic effects due to the lottery. Previously discriminated against and discouraged minorities may be emboldened to apply knowing that they stand a better chance than before. This is only speculation on my part, but commentators such as Jarvis (2008) have identified this discouragement effect. Even if this does not produce a student body which reflects the population, the fact that some minority members gain access can be seen as progress. This, I believe, is what makes some people nostalgic for the old 11-plus: although very few working class kids got into grammar schools, *some* did, and that was enough to show that grammar schools could be an escape route.

Affirmative action requires that individuals are classified, or have to classify themselves according to some norm like 'black' or 'disadvantaged'. To an abiding liberal like myself this is dangerously reminiscent of the old apartheid regime in South Africa with its race classification board. Every individual human ought to be viewed as an individual, not branded as a member of this or that category. I find it odd that few US commentators object to this form of classification. Only in the case of Lowell in San Francisco did commentators cavil at the invention of a new racial category 'east Asian' (Chinese). Can it really be the case that everyone in the US fits comfortably into a black/non-black category? These are some of the reasons why threshold lotteries for academically selective school places should at least be considered.

Having examined the specifics of threshold lotteries and the comments made about them, I now return to the whole question of tests of academic ability as selection mechanisms. This has some relevance in this chapter, where academic tests for entry to schools are being considered. It will become much more significant later when considering university entry, in particular the Dutch medical school entry system, which might be described as a weighted threshold lottery.

Shortcomings of IQ tests: Problems with tests:

You may not accept Matloff's critique of tests as selection tools in the last section, and his revulsion against race-norming, but there are other more technical problems in measuring ability by IQ. Once these have been understood perhaps a more rational basis for combing academic tests with the use of lotteries can emerge.

The evidence that tests are unfair especially to poorer children in the U.K.: A major criticism of IQ tests like the 11-plus is that they discriminate against less well-off children. A recent assessment by Atkinson, Gregg and McConnell (2006) looks at the impact of academic selection at age 11 on children in the minority of areas in England that still operate such a system:

> The answers are very clear. Overall there is little or no impact on [overall academic] attainment, but with a bigger variation between 11-plus winners and losers, than is the case in non-selective areas. This arises from the systematic under-representation of poorer children at grammar schools. The result is gains for those attending the grammar schools and a slight disadvantage for the rest. The paradox is that grammar schools bestow greater advantages to poor children than more affluent children, but very few make the cut.

This may account for the nostalgia amongst today's opinion-formers for the grammar schools. Politicians take a different view: they believe that academic testing at age 11 is socially divisive and generally ineffective in raising standards generally.

The evidence that tests unfair to specific racial groups in the U.S.: Much as social inequality based on class is the major UK obsession, so a constant theme in the US is that of racial inequality and what to do about it. The predicament in the US is that some racial groups score higher or lower, on average, than others on tests, are so are under- (or over-)represented in any school which uses selective entry based on these tests. This is so well established that it hardly needs reinforcing with evidence (see Jencks et al, 1998). One response to this is 'affirmative action' where a quota is set for each racial group.

Arbitrary and inconsistent cut-off point on entry tests: Inter-temporal fairness: I have already alluded to the extremes of the old English 11-plus where somewhere between 10% and 60% 'passed' to go to Grammar school, depending on the LEA. This was not because some counties had a much higher or lower proportion of academically gifted pupils. It was merely the result of varying provision (or a 'post-code lottery' as newspaper headlines would put it these days).

But should the highest scoring applicant always get preference? Matloff (1995) contests the whole basis of 'highest score wins' like this:

> The answer to this question requires a critical examination of just what is meant by 'best qualified.' First, one must keep in mind that neither SAT scores nor any other numeric measure will be a very accurate predictor of future grades. It thus makes no sense to admit one applicant over another simply because the first applicant had slightly higher test scores. Sadly, many of the students (and even their parents) do not see it this way. They view it like the Olympics, where being a 0.1 of a second faster can mean gold instead of silver. But what on Earth is the relevance of the Olympics to school admissions? Many students who complain about affirmative action

in university admission policies feel that higher SAT scores give one some inherent 'right' to admission to a famous school.

But when I ask whether they take advantage of the special virtues of such a school — do they attend the public lectures by world figures who visit, do they make use of the extensive library facilities, do they make it a point to take courses from Nobel laureates -- the answer is almost invariably no. On the contrary, these students usually admit that they simply want the prestigious name that the school offers. With such a confession, they clearly lose any right to the moral high ground they claim on the basis of something like SAT scores.

Another inconsistency could arise because of the arbitrary cut-off scores for entry. It might well happen that a score of 120 would be sufficient to gain a place at grammar school this year. Would it be fair to demand at least a score of 130 the following year because more applied? If a score shows that a candidate has the potential to succeed then it is ridiculous and unfair to raise this threshold because there are more applicants subsequently. The case for a cut-off corresponding to the lowest previously acceptable threshold seems unanswerable. Using a lottery to deal with the consequence of an excess of qualified applicants over places available seems nothing more than a matter of inter-generational justice, as well as good educational practice.

Misunderstanding the non-deterministic (fuzzy) relationship IQ vs. Performance: The score on an IQ test is a good indicator of future academic performance. It is easy to think of the relationship as a simple linear one. As the score on a test increases then the predicted performance, usually taken to be ability to perform in examinations at a later stage, can be expected to increase. So it seems sensible to select the highest scorers at because they can be predicted to do best in the future.

So given a choice of two candidates with differing scores then the right academic strategy would be to choose the higher scorer. Perhaps only in the 'pathological' case where two candidates have exactly the same score would a lottery be indicated. The school can always expect better results by choosing the top scorers. This simple logic hides some extra layers of complexity.

Of course, most people are aware that measurement is not an exact science, and there will be fuzziness due to many factors. There are two kinds of measurement problems that beset this reassuring model that IQ scores predict future performance. The first is that measuring IQ is subject to variability. Candidates could score better or worse if asked to take the test again on another day. The second problem is that even if the measured IQ was correct, it does not ensure the final predicted performance as shown by the relationship. Because of the fuzziness of the relationship some future 'failures' will slip through. It also means that some good candidates who could have performed as well as some those who passed will be rejected. Raising the entry threshold reduces that risk for the selectors, but applicants lose out with many being rejected despite still having a realistic chance of succeeding.

In selective systems where there is a fixed quota of entrants the selectors have to use some arbitrary score as the dividing line between pass and fail, in or out. This was what happened in the old English and Welsh 11-plus IQ test. According to Vernon (1957) the strict cut-off point meant that many children were sent to the 'wrong' type of school. Because of the uncertainties in the measurement process, it was estimated that 20 percent of pupils finished up in a Grammar school when they should have been at a Secondary Modern or vice versa.

Borderzones: The implementation of the 11-plus test varied from one LEA to another. It was appreciated that the test was not perfect, and that a sharp cut-off point would result in the unfairness of candidates being wrongly allocated. For this reason most LEAs adopted a 'border zone' procedure, calling for further reports on candidates who fell just below the cut-off point. As time went on this border zone shrank, mainly for practical reasons. What was needed, according to one shrewd local councillor, was a test which was "technically sound, administratively feasible and politically defensible" (Vernon 1957, p. 30). The IQ test seemed to be sound. For administrative and political reasons the border zone was progressively shrunk.

It was just such an argument that led me (Boyle, 1998) to propose a much wider border-zone, perhaps including up to 50 percent of all applicants, who would then be subject to random selection, but with their chances weighted according to the points scored. In a comment on my paper, Barbara Goodwin observed that "In justice, there ought to be a lottery for *all* candidates." This would make the lottery-selection process into something much more complex, which would need a lot of explaining to the public. The simplicity of 'borderline point-scorers go into the lucky dip' is attractive. I will return to more complex weighted systems in Chapter 8 on the Dutch medical school entry lottery, where issues of justice and efficiency will be explored further.

Non-linearity: A further complication in the use of IQ scores to predict performance arises from the assumption of linearity. Since this is of little relevance to selection for school places I leave this topic for now. Later in Chapter 9 I explore the implications of non-linearity when examining the idea of using a lottery for university entrance.

Conclusion Using measurements of innate ability such as IQ tests is without doubt the best way for academically selective schools to choose their entrants. But such tests are not perfect. They are unfair to some races and classes. Some children can gain an unwarranted advantage by coaching. Cut-off points will vary for no defensible academic reason, only the capacity of the school. As with all tests errors will be made leading to considerable mis-classification of winners and losers. When all of these inevitable shortcomings of tests are accepted then the case for some application of lottery choosing to the borderline candidates seems obvious.

Chapter 7

University Entrance by Lottery: Judging Merit

Don't believe everything you read in newspapers! When the top headline in the *Sunday Times* was: **Universities to pick students by lottery** (Sep 6, 2003) this was just speculation or 'kite-flying' as it is called by political commentators. True, there was a major review of English higher education admissions procedures underway, under the chairmanship of Professor Stephen Schwartz. It had been looking at some of the lottery-based admissions systems in use, particularly the one used for medical school entry in the Netherlands. There will be much more about this marvel of Dutch pragmatism in the next chapter. But no, the Schwartz commission was not about to emulate, or rather anticipate the schools admissions code and recommend random selection. In their final Report (Schwartz, 2004a) *Fair admissions to higher education* they made no suggestions about using a lottery.

Admissions to universities and schools differ fundamentally from each other. Schools on the one hand are set up to cater for all the children in the population with a standard curriculum. Once schools have non-selective entry (like most in England and Wales), and when parental choice is added on, then admissions by lottery may seem a reasonable way to treat all applicants equally in a non-discriminatory manner. Colleges and especially universities on the other hand are academic establishments so some form of academic selection is inevitable. To throw higher education courses open to all-comers and then resolve the excess demand by a lottery would be unthinkable.

Lottery-admission exists nonetheless, and was even being considered as a means of picking winners for English university places. But is lottery-admission yet another example of well-intentioned moves towards equality of opportunity resulting in some strange deformations of higher education? Deciding who should be admitted to study on vital vocational courses like law and medicine by the luck of the draw seems to be the height of folly. Despite that, in this chapter and the next one I hope to show that *in appropriate circumstances* a lottery can be an excellent adjunct the process of admitting students onto courses.

In the old days, getting onto a university course always required some minimum qualification such as Matriculation. In some countries, most notably Italy, all qualified candidates were entitled to enrol on any course at any university. This led to huge numbers of students, sometimes in their thousands, crowding on to popular courses. Ability to pay fees and support one-self was another means of limiting numbers which applied in my own student days in Ireland in the 1960s. The 'affordability' hurdle was removed for many by the introduction of student grants and subsidised or free tuition. This in turn creates more demand for places. For courses such as medicine and engineering, where laboratory or workshop availability restricts numbers, then some means of rationing the available places is needed.

Decidedly inappropriate methods have been used in the past: places on some courses were reserved for pupils from favoured schools. This applied to some Oxbridge colleges when admitting public school candidates. Nepotism or other insider preferences can sometimes lead to preferential admissions. Priority may be given to applicants whose father had also attended the particular degree course or university. This still exists as a perk of the job for Faculty members at US Ivy League universities, whereby their children get preferential entry (Traub, 2005).

It is possible to imagine a market-based system for university entry, with the authorities charging what the market will bear for degree courses. This almost seems to be the case for MBAs! Robert Klitgaard (1985) goes one stage further and carries out a thought-experiment. He imagines a time in the future when Harvard (his university) still retains its elite status, but chooses to auction off its places to suitably qualified applicants by a system of closed bids. He recognises that elitism is akin to the dogma of the market: that if something is highly valuable then people will be prepared to pay, not just for its cost of production but whatever scarcity value the product might possess. But this is only an amusing hypothetical aside which aims to show the nonsense of letting the market decide the award of university places. In his little parable, Klitgaard reminds us that universities, even elite ones, cannot exist in some purified market place. They are part of society and must contribute accordingly. Rejection of a free-market alternative can go some way towards justifying the use of lotteries.

'Merit' remains the universally acceptable criterion which is used to decide who gets in and who gets rejected when university courses are over-subscribed. How this Merit can be measured, and what counts as *appropriate* Merit will be examined in the second half of this chapter. This should help clarify when a lottery might have a useful part to play in the selection process.

Examples of lottery use in college and university admissions: These range from minor uses which only affect a small number of marginal applicants, to lottery procedures in which all qualified candidates are either accepted or rejected, randomly.

(27) Borderline selection, National University of Ireland (NUI) 2009: The first example applies academic selection criteria with a very limited use of the lottery. For NUI courses[7] a strict grade criterion is used with no other selection procedures. Scores (points) above a pre-ordained level lead to definite acceptance, below that grade is rejection. In the borderline grade it is almost inevitable that there will be an excess of applicants over places still available. As

---

[7] I should declare an interest here: my first degree in Engineering in 1964 was from University College, Dublin, a constituent college of NUI. My sole requirement for entry was a Pass in the Irish Leaving Certificate, with Honours in Maths. All qualified applicants were accepted, so long as they paid their fees.

the NUI website explains (from www.nuim.ie): "The University distinguishes between applicants on equal points scores by appending to each score a randomly-generated number. The combined score/random number is the final determinant of position in order of merit."

This seems eminently fair to all of those who fall into the border-zone. They all have equal numbers of points (or fall within a band which is deemed equivalent), but at the lowest level at which students are to be accepted on a course.

(28) Shortlisting, QMC Medical School, London 2003: This is a one-off example, but the detail is highly informative, so I will let Jon Fuller head of graduate entry at the Queen Mary school of medicine and dentistry explain why it has become the first college to use a lottery to draw up a short-list from all the qualified applicants. (*The Times,* Sep 14, 2003)

> Earlier this year I was faced with a seemingly impossible task. More than 1,200 people had applied to train as a doctor on the graduate entry programme at Queen Mary college in London – for just 40 places. How on earth could I choose between them?
>
> Checking through their forms, my heart sank. Around half were apparently qualified to start the course. What about the 26-year-old with a masters degree in pharmacy, three years' experience as a pharmacist and a glowing reference from his academic supervisor? Or the 30-year-old PhD in maths with a BSc in sports science who had done voluntary work with disadvantaged children. She, too, had a positive reference from her academic supervisor. Not to mention the 32-year-old man with a BSc in optometry who worked as an optometrist in a hospital, wanted to be an ophthalmic surgeon and had done voluntary work with adults with chronic illnesses. Which one would you have chosen for interview?
>
> Fortunately, the medical school, anticipating a possible avalanche of applications this year, had recently taken a radical decision. We had decided to whittle the 650 who met our entry criteria down to 120 potential interviewees – on purely random grounds.

Tomorrow, the first set of students selected partly by what headline writers have already called a 'lottery' will start training to be doctors at Queen Mary. All successful applicants must have achieved a first-class honours degree or a 2:1 in a science subject. They have to have a positive reference from a colleague or teacher, they have to show evidence of knowing what a career in medicine means and they have to pass a psychometric test, the Personal Qualities Assessment.

Looking at the 650 that met all those criteria it was difficult to distinguish them from each other. Ucas forms are not always helpful when choosing between applicants. Instead we chose to select 120 randomly and interview them in detail to find the 40 needed; (each applicant was interviewed by four pairs of interviewers and asked to comment on a video of a patient consulting a doctor).

On the reactions to random short-listing, Fuller goes on:

We are the first medical school in this country that has explicitly used random selection, and we have had approval and criticism in equal parts. Many candidates have been understanding; I have spoken to applicants and parents who can see the logic of our procedures.

But many not picked were bitterly disappointed and remain angry with us. I am still dealing with the flak from their complaints to MPs, the General Medical Council and Ucas, the universities admissions service.

Yet random selection is a method that has been used for entry to higher education elsewhere in Europe, such as in the Netherlands, for many years. I must emphasise that random selection is only part of our selection procedure. Colleagues from other medical schools have been supportive, although many have told me that we were brave to admit that we used random selection. They understand because the problems we faced last year are not confined to Queen Mary.

We have been criticised for excluding people who would make good doctors. This is true, but it would be true whatever method we used. But at least, with our method, exclusion for the majority is not a criticism of them or their potential. But when people say that a lottery is no way to choose doctors; I respond, then tell me, faced with these numbers of talented and qualified candidates – what is?

Alternatives to random short-listing

Some universities, faced with even more overwhelming numbers of excellent applicants – such as Cambridge – have instituted further exams in order to rank their applicants academically. The problem of distinguishing graduate entry applicants who want to train as doctors is even greater than that for students applying straight from A-levels, since the range of experience and qualifications is greater.

Unlike Cambridge, we decided not to raise the academic standards even higher, not to set any more exams (they had already demonstrated academic qualities) and not to use discriminators such as age or social class. Most undergraduate medical schools, including Queen Mary, select by reading Ucas forms and predicted A-level results, deciding from what is written whether to interview. Applicants are given a 15-minute interview (Queen Mary interviewed 1,000 A-level applicants last year). We know some applicants are coached and personal statements written for them.

The kernel of this process is that 650 extremely well-qualified candidates are whittled down to 120 by a lottery. These survivors were then subjected to intensive scrutiny from which just 40 survive to be accepted onto the course. There is very little risk to QMC of accepting a 'dud' in this process. They also gain from not having to spend time interviewing and testing the 530 'lottery losers' (650 minus 120) who are all admittedly well-qualified candidates and yet are rejected at random. It is greatly to be hoped that these 530 rejects find suitable alternative occupations, and have not wasted their efforts in acquiring such high qualifications. At least they will know that their rejection is not a sign of inadequacy, only the result of an impartial random decision.

Examples of lotteries selecting from all qualified applicants:
In all of the following examples applicants must meet some minimum standard to be eligible for the draw, but once the applicant is selected by the lottery they are on the course. No further tests or interviews are applied.

(29) Glendale Nursing College, California 1997 onwards: This example is similar to the threshold lotteries described in the last chapter. It caught my eye because of the vociferous condemnation it attracted. But first here is what the current (2009) website (*www.glendale.edu*) says about getting into Glendale Nursing:

> The formula [based on test scores in a range of relevant subjects] produces a score reflecting the percent likelihood that a student will be successful in the nursing program. Using these criteria will help us enroll students who are most likely to complete the program and help alleviate our severe nursing shortage.
>
> This formula resulted from a state-wide study involving more than 5,000 nursing students in over 20 community college districts. The pool of eligible applicants resulting from this method is very strong academically. However, there are still too many applicants for the seats available. By law we are not allowed to apply any more criteria at this point and all selected students must be chosen randomly – we use the lottery. We draw names and fill our seats in order that the names are selected from this eligible pool of applicants.

So places ('seats' is the American jargon) are allocated randomly, without any further discrimination to all qualified applicants. No extra weighting is given to high-scorers. It is re-assuring to read that they base their choice of cut-off score from the results of "a state-wide study". Such rationality is rare amongst administrators of selection processes!

But are Glendale right to use a lottery? My attention was drawn to this particular use of lottery-selection by an article by Ted Rueter in *The Christian Science Monitor* (Dec 12, 1997)

> **When Good Grades Don't Count** [..] The celebration of mediocrity is in full bloom at [Glendale College, which] has instituted a lottery system for admission to its nursing program. This semester, 38 names were pulled at random from 156 'qualified applicants' – those with at least C averages in core courses.
>
> According to the chancellor of California's community colleges, grade point averages are an 'artificial barrier' to professional school admission. "We can't discriminate in favor of students who get A's

> over students who may be getting B's," says Mary Parker, dean of
> nursing at Cuesta. "Just because you have straight A's doesn't mean
> you're going to be a good nurse." Parker also maintains that
> distinguishing among GPAs is impossible, given that a C student
> may be a single mother holding down a full-time job, while the A
> student may be a 19-year-old full-time student living with her
> parents. [..]

So far so reasonable; a straightforward description and justification
of Glendale's lottery selection process. But later in the article the
tone changes:

> There is substantial anti-elitism in American life. Job applicants are
> rejected for being 'overeducated' or 'overqualified.'..... The
> intellectually inclined are dismissed as 'eggheads.' ....Many college
> students wear Homer Simpson T-shirts: 'Underachiever and proud
> of it.' ... Others are not so contemptuous of meritocracy. Susan Jolly,
> an A student at Glendale College who didn't win the admissions
> lottery, complains, "You work so hard for so long, to get really good
> grades in really hard classes. Then you find out it doesn't matter."

Clearly the author of this article in the *Christian Science Monitor* is
confused: a meritocratic society is not necessarily one which
awards the prizes to those who perform best on tests. 'Merit' and
test scores are related, but they are not identical as I will show later
in this chapter. It is simply not the case that places on nursing
courses should automatically go to those with highest grades. "Just
because you have straight A's doesn't mean you're going to be a
good nurse" as the Dean of nursing studies observed (above).

**(30) Physiotherapy at Leeds Metropolitan and Huddersfield 2004:
Random selection with quotas:** Two English universities have
chosen a similar procedure for admissions onto physiotherapy
courses to that adopted by Glendale, but with an extra twist: there
are quotas for different categories of applicant. This is how the
scheme was reported (*BBC News*, Mar 27, 2004):

> Two West Yorkshire universities have admitted they use a lottery
> system to choose between applicants for heavily over-subscribed
> courses: Leeds Metropolitan and Huddersfield universities have both

introduced computer generated 'random selection' for their physiotherapy courses. About 20 applications are received for every place on the course. The universities say the system is the fairest way to give A-level pupils an equal chance of admission. Professor Simon Lee, the vice-chancellor of Leeds Metropolitan said: "If we whittled it down to those who've done terrifically well at school, they've shown an interest in it, they've got an aptitude for it...we've still got 600 people for 40 places. [..] we are passionately committed to fairness."

But Tom Wong, the communications officer for the students' union at Leeds disagreed:

"For students' futures to be decided on a lottery is totally unacceptable. It cheapens the concept of education and makes a mockery of 'fairness' in the current system. If universities are over-subscribed then each and every able applicant should be taken through a thorough application procedure. This is simply laziness on the part of the universities."

The extra twist in this story is the application of quotas for male, female and mature students. According to reports in *The Times* and the *Huddersfield Daily Examiner* (both Mar 28, 2004) Gill Robinson, Huddersfield admissions tutor, explained that there were 900 applications for 50 physiotherapy places. The university chose the 600 of these who were predicted to get at least three C grades at A-level. She then divided applications into three piles: mature students, men and women. Applicants were then chosen at random from the piles to get the right balance between the groups. "People throw their hands up in horror," she said "but we don't have a better alternative."

It is not clear why the quota system was in operation. It *may* have been a means of producing a 'balanced' intake, when applications from, say, men were fewer than hoped for, and this produced the desired mix. If this was so then it could surely be challenged as unfair. Alternatively, perhaps a misguided fear that the outcome of lottery-selection would be, say, a freshman year which was 100 percent female that led the organisers to impose this diversity-ensuring mechanism.

While in theory it is possible to anticipate a highly perverse lottery result, in practice it is so remote that it can be safely ignored. I argued this point with Barnett (1998), co-author of *The Athenian Option*. He felt a randomly selected House of Lords had to be 50/50 men and women, and only quotas would ensure this. But the chances of even a mildly skewed assembly of 650 randomly picked peers, say 55/45 is miniscule. And where do the quotas stop? If quotas for gender, why not for religious affinity, sexual orientation, dis-ability and any other sub-group with sufficient clout to demand proportional representation? The beauty of the lottery is that it is completely blind, being oblivious to *all* variations, whether they are acknowledged or not, and can generally be relied upon to produce a result proportional to the population from which it is drawn.

Currently (2009) neither university makes any mention of a lottery in their course details. There was some suggestion in 2004 when this story broke that Ucas, the centralised university-place clearing agency would not approve. It might also be that the universities have continued with the practice, but without making too much fuss about it.

Another example from the Netherlands (31) B.Sc. Business, Maastricht, Netherlands 2009: I say "another" because there will be a whole chapter describing the notorious Netherlands weighted lottery scheme for medical school entry. This scheme, at the University of Maastricht Faculty of Economics and Business Administration is more straightforward, and involves admission to the Bachelor of Science Programmes specialising in International Business: (from *www.fdewb.unimaas.nl*)

> The number of places available for the International Business programme is limited to 400 (the so-called *numerus fixus*). If the number of applicants exceeds the available capacity, a central selection by lottery takes place for 200 places. The remaining 200 will be allocated through the faculty's decentralised selection procedures.

Selecting students:
A lottery is not a substitute for selection on Merit

From the many comments on the lottery-entry schemes described above, you get the feeling that there is something dubious about the use of random selection. Given the urgent press of hard-working, well-qualified applicants it is surely a dereliction of duty on the part of the admissions tutors to reject many of them by the fickle process of a lot. Is it not laziness on the part of faculty staff who do not make the effort and spend enough time to consider the merits of each and every candidate in full? Opting for a lottery looks like a quick and easy dodge. I do not for one moment disagree with the principle that Merit alone should determine university entrance. Rather it is the form of merit used that I would disagree with.

Under the guise of this seemingly benign and inarguable concept, several inappropriate, not to say wrong forms of measuring Merit have crept in. One major justification for the use of lotteries is that it blocks *all* forms of rationality, preventing good reasons as well as bad ones. Using bad reasons leads to a version of selection that could be called 'false merit'. I will try to point out what are the false forms of merit and why they should they should be blocked – preferably by lottery.

On their own the use of lotteries for admissions process would also preclude the good reasons, what might be called 'valid merit'. It is just as important to identify valid merit. The decision to accept or reject applicants should be based on that alone. So the principle might be: apply the good reasons to measure valid merit and use a lottery to prevent false merit.

The origins of Meritocracy: Prior to meritocracy, posts and places were awarded by patronage, nepotism, simony (patronage is when the post is in the gift of a patron, the classic example being Church of England incumbencies for vicars; nepotism is the award of jobs to family relatives; simony is the procuring of church offices for money) and other curious means.

Parkinson (1958) of 'Parkinson's Law' fame described the introduction of competitive examinations for Civil Service entry as about the best system ever invented for selecting competent employees. He was in a position to know having been employed as a respected management consultant. The word 'meritocracy' was famously coined about the same time as Parkinson's Law by Michael Young in his 1958 social satire *The Rise of Meritocracy 1870 – 2033: an essay in education and equality*. The date – 1870 – was when the Trevelyan reforms of Civil Service involving exam-based entry were introduced.

Young predicted that over-reliance on the admittedly highly reliable Intelligence Quotient (IQ) tests to allocate children to different schools would lead to the stratification of society. In the end, by the year 2033 the proletariat would rise up against their helotry of the stupid. Young was not entirely correct in his interpretation of IQ tests, as I will explain in the next section. Although both of these books were intended to be humorous, they both had a serious intent and reached a wide and influential audience.

Despite Young's warning, meritocracy is still seen as the model for a better society, where hard-working individuals are allowed to thrive on their merits rather than on who they know, or worse, who their parents were. 'Selection on merit' is widely accepted, particularly in educational circles as the highest ideal.

Although 'merit' could be an abstract philosophical concept, Young did not hesitate in producing a formula for it:

$$\mathbf{M = I + E} \text{ (where M is Merit, I is measured IQ, E is effort)}$$

Young produced masses of evidence for the use of IQ testing as the best and most reliable indicator of success on academic courses, but also in all forms of employment and other fields of endeavour. He assumed that measuring IQ would become more reliable over time, all the better to closely identify the necessary talent. As to the second part of Young's formula, Effort, he was on less certain ground. He alludes to the practices of work study engineers and assumes that they have (or soon would have) a precise science of measuring effort.

Young probably never meant that his formula to be taken too literally; this is a satire after all. Scientists might quibble about the simple additive model he proposed, but the two components are surely valid. Using IQ or some near equivalent — grades in school-leaving examinations are the usual marker for university entrance — is supported by ample evidence. The higher the entry grade the better the predicted performance. This is as true now as it was in 1958 when Young produced his book on Meritocracy. What has not changed though is the uncertainty in the relationship. Young's assumption that measures like IQ would become less error-prone has not happened. Predicting performance based on entry scores remains an inexact science, but it is still a very good, perhaps the only valid reason for selecting some and rejecting others. As will be seen, no other measure comes anywhere near to reliably identifying Merit.

The second part of his formula was probably a catch-all item to counter the oft-heard argument that we all know some very clever people who are bone idle. How could it be said they possess Merit? Young was aware of the activities of work-study engineers and assumed that they had cracked the problem of measuring Effort. In reality their measures of effort were, and still remain a highly subjective activity based on human judgement. It is from the dubious attempt to measure Young's 'Effort' that many of the bad reasons for selection originate.

The conventional means of selection by universities: In practice, for colleges and universities, selection on merit becomes a bureaucratic procedure where the element of merit may be determined by objective criteria (such as a test, or score on an examination), but much is often left to the discretion of the selectors. I am sure that readers are familiar with the standard procedure of application form — screening — short-listing. This may lead directly to offers of places. For more elite courses there may be further tests. But above all else it is the interview which is the centrepiece of the academic selection ritual.

Greely (1977) describes a particularly elaborate system used for entry to Yale University Law School. Three thousand applications are made for the 325 places available. Each application is read and ranked by three faculty members. It is relatively easy, he claims, to identify the top and bottom candidates. The real problem comes in spotting who fits into the 250th to 350th category, where differences in 'merit' will be insignificant. Attempting to pick the 'best' candidates is not just a costly business, it is in Greely's description a "pretense". He goes on to point out that random selection would be the fairest and cheapest method.

False Merit: I will look two conventional techniques which purport to identify merit and explain why they should not be used.

Second order merit: A technique for distinguishing merit it to ask about outside activities, such as prowess at sport, membership of clubs, charitable activities and other contributions to the community. While these are without doubt meritorious and they also show evidence of effort, should they be used to decide who is admitted or rejected? If the criterion is simply to predict who is likely to perform best on a course, then the answer must be 'no'. Of course if it can be shown that those with sporting ability really *are* better equipped to succeed then it can be promulgated and used to decide marginal cases.

If admissions tutors are to ignore evidence of 'good works' this of course removes any incentive to carry out such meritorious activity. But what, one might ask, is the merit in doing good solely to earn merit awards? Another perverse incentive is that performance of such good works is notoriously difficult to check, and so the incentive to make them up becomes difficult to resist.

A consequence of this form of merit selection is what is described as 'grade inflation' – when more and more students get straight A-grades how do elite universities select the 'best'? As Tim Harford the 'Undercover Economist' at the *Financial Times* puts it (Mar 20, 2009):

Grade distortion [inflation] is a serious affair. Students and their teachers are forced to switch to grey market transactions denominated in alternative currencies: the letter of recommendation, for example. Like most alternative currencies, these are a hassle. Grade distortions, like price distortions, destroy information and oblige people to look in strange places for some signal amid the noise. Students are judged not on their strongest subjects – A grade, of course – but on whether they also picked up A grades in their weakest. When excellence cannot be displayed, plaudits go instead to those who deliver pat answers without stumbling – politicians in training, presumably.

So is the answer a finer grading system so that the candidates with really tip-top grades can be identified? Or is the 'grey market currency' of good works and specific subjects to be the final arbiter? Faced with these conundrums, perhaps the use of a lottery does not look so outrageous.

The ineffectiveness of interviews: Having winnowed the applicant field down by picking those with the best predicted grades as well as a glittering array of 'good works' there may still be a surplus of applicants. Conventionally the next stage is to interview these survivors and allow 'expert' judgement to decide who is best suited to the course. Since the interview is often the core technique for deciding who has the most 'merit' its effectiveness should be scrutinised closely.

Evidence of the ineffectiveness of interviewing as a means of selecting students was given by Steven Schwartz (2004b) in a submission to the House of Commons select committee on education: He is quoted as saying "..interviews take place at some of our most ancient universities, and the reliability of these interviews is zero". He referred to an experiment in Kelman & Canger (1994) where veterinarian applicants were selected, half with by an interview, half at random. Judging by the results at the end of the course, it was impossible to distinguish between the two groups. "To me, it [selecting by interview] is the same as flipping a coin." (I feel Schwartz was using this as a rhetorical device rather than as a policy prescription). Claims by admission tutors that their records showed that they were able to pick out high-flyer were dismissed as "an illusion".

A further problem related to interviews and other subjective selection techniques is that of discrimination. It would be wrong, and against university policy if admissions tutors were for example, to actively prefer attractive young white female applicants over others who were equally qualified. This is an agency problem, and however well-intentioned, it is difficult to control this bias. Public Choice theory would assume that selectors would act in this discriminatory way for their own convenience, if they are given the discretion to do so.

Even where selectors are acting with best intentions, and even following training to avoid such discrimination, it is still difficult to avoid unwitting bias. Beyond the recognised forms of discrimination on grounds of gender, race, age and perhaps sexual orientation there are many more human traits and features which either help or hinder candidates in interviews. It may seem trivial to cite handedness (left or right), short height, obesity or baldness as characteristics which affect a candidates chances, but there is evidence that they do (in Boyle 2006).

Interviews are often conducted by 'amateurs', people who may be expert in their chosen field of say, medicine, but have no specific expertise in judging the suitability of applicants for courses. It might be expected that schoolteachers with longstanding knowledge of their pupils could reliably predict their pupils performance. Not so. According to Vernon (1957) the predictive ability of the teachers was invariably worse than the 'quick and dirty' 11-plus test of intelligence. Camerer (p 611-2, in Kagel & Roth 1995) puts it more directly:

> A body of literature concerns judgments made repeatedly by people (many of them experts) in natural settings where stochastic outcomes depend on some observable predictors (e.g., test scores) and some unobservables. Examples include medical or psychiatric diagnosis (severity of Hodgkins' disease, schizophrenia), predictions of recidivism or parole violation by criminals, ratings of marital happiness, and bankruptcy of firms. About 100 careful studies have

been documented so far. The remarkable finding in almost all these studies is that weighted linear combinations of observables predict outcomes better than individual experts can.

In a study by Dawes (1971) it was discovered that academic success of doctoral students could be predicted better by a sum of three measures – GRE scores, a rating of the quality of the student's undergraduate school, and her undergraduate grades. These were better than the ratings of a faculty admissions committee. To put it bluntly, the faculty's deliberation just added noise to calculation based on the three measures. The only documented exceptions to the general conclusion that models consistently out-predict experts are found in a few kinds of esoteric medical diagnosis.

In studies of experts making judgements, they are routinely found to violate rational expectations by using observable information less efficiently than simple numerical models. The violations have two common forms:

(1) experts often add extra error into predictions when they use complicated interactions of variables (weighting grades from low-quality schools more heavily, for example), rather than more robust linear combinations of variables;

(2) Variables are known to be weakly predictive of outcomes (personal interviews, for example) are given too much attention by experts when they should be ignored. These psychological tendencies can be traced to some of the judgment biases discussed above.

The interview is generally the ultimate decider of who has 'merit'. In reality it merely reflects the prejudices, witting or unwitting of the interviewer. It is on this basis that a lottery becomes not just acceptable, but a more just, even a more efficient process than the highly flawed interviews that are usually the final arbiter of merit. Using a lottery to block this form of specious reasoning seems entirely justified.

It may be difficult to convince highly intelligent members of faculty that they have no useful skills in judging character in the interview room. We all believe that we are good or at least above average car drivers; so too does ability to judge character seem to be assumed, despite the evidence to the contrary. At the very least those who advocate interviewing should be required to produce the evidence that it works. Otherwise a lottery is the positive alternative: it works, it is cheap and quick but above all it should be seen to be fair.

So Merit equals test scores? Not quite:

SAT scores or IQ points are not yet 'merit'. Test scores as we saw in the last chapter are generally closely related to Intelligence which as Young was at great pains to point out is an excellent indicator of Merit. For our purposes that would mean the ability to succeed in a chosen course of studies. So looking for candidates with the highest test scores is an entirely rational and sound strategy to adopt. Basing selection on a lottery alone and ignoring test scores would be quite wrong.

But what if there is an excess of top-scoring candidates, all with straight A-grades? Should there be more tests with finer gradations in the scoring system (marks out of 1000 rather than percentages out of 100)? This can, and sometimes is carried through, but it is probably futile. All test scores are subject to measurement error. That doesn't mean they are wrong or mistaken; it is just a normal feature of measurement. Finer grading does not overcome this inherent inaccuracy. In a grades-based system (as in the National University of Ireland example (27) above) it seems entirely appropriate to apply a lottery to those in the borderline grade.

There is a further point about grades which I will return to in the next chapter: in respect of university courses is it always true the higher grades indicate students more likely, not just to succeed on their chosen course, but go on to be competent professionals? Instead perhaps Merit ought be measured by *adequate* grades for the chosen course, an idea that was directly stated in the Glendale Nursing College example (29) above. So grades matter, and should be taken into account, but it is not necessarily the case of the higher the better. What is needed is to identify what level makes an applicant *eligible* to be considered for entry. When there are more eligible candidates than places then the case for using a lottery becomes more compelling.

What is left of 'Merit'? So the two parts of Young's formula for Merit are flawed. Intelligence can be measured and gives some indication of likely future performance. Effort as identified by interview is almost completely useless, and should never be used. Additional information about good works is equally flawed. The case for an alternative in the form of threshold lottery selection amongst eligible candidates seems sound. It can be improved upon with a weighted combination of entry scores and a lottery as will be seen in the next chapter. But the basic tenet remains that Valid Merit can only be based on test scores. All else is false merit.

What the *Admissions to Higher Education Review* said: This was published under the title *Fair admissions to higher education: recommendations for good practice* (Schwartz, 2004a). It contains no mention of exotic instruments such as the lottery. Instead it produced five rather bland principles for fair admissions.

> Principle 1: A fair admissions system should be transparent.
>
> Principle 2: A fair admissions system should enable institutions to select students who are able to complete the course as judged by their achievements and their potential.
>
> Principle 3: A fair admissions system should strive to use assessment methods that are reliable and valid.
>
> Principle 4: A fair admissions system should seek to minimise barriers for applicants.
>
> Principle 5: A fair admissions system should be professional in every respect and underpinned by appropriate institutional structures and processes.

There is little to disagree with in all this, but it hardly gives much specific detail for admissions tutors to work with either! The word 'merit' is used repeatedly throughout the Report, but interpreted in many different ways.

Interviews are not excluded either, but buried in a footnote on p.39 is the evidence:

In an overview of literature relating to the validity of medical school interviews, Ferguson, James and Madeley (2002) conclude that interviews can provide "useful additional information that has predictive power for outcome" (p.956). Kreiter, Yin, Solow and Brennan (2004) test the reproducibility of interview scores (again for admission to medical school) and conclude that interviews are not reliable. See, too, Patterson, Lane, Ferguson and Norfolk (2001) for description of a competency-based selection system for general practitioner registrars in which structured interviews are judged to help to elicit useful information.

Note that Schwartz's reference before the Commons Select Committee to Kelman & Canger (1994) was not produced here. The use of 'structured interviews' is thus held to have *some* validity in the selection process.

Chapter 8

The Dutch Weighted Lottery: Practical Politics

"The bizarre Dutch system" Here's how Professor Piet Drenth (1999) opens his description:

> For decades the system of selection of medical students has been the subject of lively debate both in the professional and the popular press in the Netherlands. The discussions have often had an emotional and political undercurrent; emotional, because a good many applicants for medical studies have been and will be disappointed, since only about one third of the total group of often highly motivated applicants can be admitted to one of the medical faculties each year, and political since opinions differ widely as to the choice between the two seemingly incompatible goals: free choice of study for those who qualify themselves according to the rules, on the one hand, and the selection of those students who have the best chance of success in the medical study, on the other.

This dilemma is not just a Dutch problem one of course, it is a universal one. Are we to allow universities to choose freely only those best suited for a course or should all qualified applicant-customers be given the freedom to choose whatever course they wish to attend? There will always be limited numbers of places available on some courses, so when there are more applicants than places, who should win the prize, and who should be the losers? The problem becomes especially acute for the ever-popular medical, veterinary and dentistry courses.

There had been suggestions from writers in the US and Canada that a lottery might be the best way to resolve the problems of over-subscription for courses in medicine (Simpson, 1975; DeWitt, 1971), but it was the Dutch who took the bold step of doing it. Not without some criticism, as Drenth notes. In the press outside the Netherlands the 'Dutch solution' has been subject of deliberation and wonder, with one particular aspect, the weighted lottery being referred to as "the bizarre Dutch system of allocating places for over-subscribed university courses through a computerised tombola" (*'in a recent magazine article'*). One of the central elements of the system is that acceptance for courses is determined by a form of lottery where the chances of being admitted increase with the grade point average in the final secondary school exam is higher. (Details of this will be elaborated later in this chapter). Even in the Netherlands Drenth says that this system..

> ...is often criticised, if not reviled. Undoubtedly, a lot of these negative attitudes are based on ignorance and lack of familiarity with the backgrounds of the selection system. On the other hand, the system has its weaknesses, as is shown by the continuous recurrence of debate in the Dutch press, among experts and even in parliament.

So the Dutch system is flawed. But is it one which should be avoided, stemming as it does "from the pathological Dutch drive for fairness and their intense dislike for making tough decisions" as Drenth quotes, or is it a marvel which is so appropriate for university-place selection that it should be widely copied? Follow the explanation in this chapter, and I think you will find it is the latter. But rationality is not enough to ensure that even the best systems survive the depredations of practical politics; this too, is a theme of this chapter.

(32) Medical Schools, the Netherlands 1975 – 1998: A consequence of a rigorously streamed secondary school system is that less than 10 percent[8] of the secondary school graduates have the right to directly commence university studies, although there is wide provision for many forms of higher education in the

---

[8] Since then the proportion has risen. In 2003 it was about 16%. Central Office of Statistics NL

Netherlands. At the end of the secondary schooling stage there is a two-part examination: a nationwide examination in all subjects which the student has selected, and an achievement test prepared by the school and scored by its own teachers, but moderated by external examiners from other schools. Universities are not allowed any other screening devices (interviews, special tests, references, extra-curricular achievements). These final school results are recorded as simple scores (grades) from 1 to 10, so a score of 9.6 (out of 10) is extremely good, a score of 6.5 or less is only so-so.

Exam score	*	under 6.5	6.5-7.0	7.0-7.5	7.5-8.0	8.0-8.5	8.5 +
GRADE	G	F	E	D	C	B	A
% getting	12%	30%	22%	21%	9%	5%	2%

*G is a catch-all category for non-standard applications, for example those from outside the Netherlands. (figures from Drenth (1999))

The weighted lottery: The term 'weighted lottery' ('gewogen loting' in Dutch) is used to describe this system, although it may be more familiar to some as 'quota sampling' or 'stratified sampling'. The weighting in this form of lottery is based on academic criteria. We have previously encountered lotteries which were weighted to deliberately favour disadvantaged ethnic or social groups. In Chapter 3 there were examples from the US in Chicago (13) and Pasadena (14). The Dutch system is not like this at all; selection is on purely academic grounds. (Although Ben Wilbrink tells me that there was a proposal about 1980 from the then minister of education Arie Pais to consider the ethnic background, sex and military service of applicants, but this was never adopted)

Since the *numerus fixus* was promulgated by the Ministry of Education the three disciplines of medicine, dentistry and veterinarian studies have all experienced substantially more applicants each year than the educational capacity of the universities. Drenth reports that each year during the mid-1990s some 5,000 interested students had to compete for 1,800 places in medicine. For dentistry the ratio is somewhat more favourable, for veterinarian studies even more unfavourable.

The way the weighted lottery works is shown in the Table below: The 'SCORE' category relates to the banded grade in the results of the school-leaving examinations. The probability of success for the entry scores are not given, so I have inferred them from the data. It looks like the administrators had a target probability for winning from each of the categories with the following weightings:

SCORE Grade	G	F	E	D	C	B	A
Chance of a win	40%	25%	33%	40%	50%	60%	80%

In the official Dutch version of the Drenth (1997) Report there are many tables which show slightly different weightings from those shown here, but these represent typical values for the quotas in each category. The general model states that in cases of restricted admission, an applicant's chances of being admitted - that is, the number of lottery tickets he or she receives - is a monotonically increasing function of his or her secondary school grade point average. This model thus falls between a straight threshold lottery selection scheme and one which awards places to the highest scorers first.[9]

The actual selection procedure is as follows: Students who wish to attend one of the medical studies courses must submit their application to a central clearing-house. Their application will then receive a randomly assigned number, the lower the number the greater the chance of success. In subsequent correspondence with Professor Drenth (Aug 2000) he tells me that these numbers used to be derived from random number tables, with a 'notary lawyer' who is employed by the ministry allocating the numbers. This is not then a public draw, but so far, Drenth tells me, no-one has

---

[9] You can follow the methodology of the weighting scheme from the original administrative documents, together with some statistical arguments about their interpretation (in Dutch) at: http://www.benwilbrink.nl/publicaties/ 75GewogenLotingCOWO.htm

questioned the honesty or integrity of the process or the official involved.

Applicants will know their numbers in advance, so can form some view about their prospects of winning, depending, of course, on the Grade they achieve in their final school examinations. Elsewhere (*Times Higher Educational Supplement*, Jul 19, 1996) there is reference to an agency called IMG in Groeningen which implements university student selection including the provision of random numbers, and so, is in effect, running the draw. Currently (2010) this is called IB-Groep. Information for students can be found at their website at *www.ib-groep.nl/ particulieren/ studeren/ loten.*

There are further aspects of the system which was in use between 1975 and 1998 that should be pointed out:

–Applicants were allowed an unlimited number of attempts in the yearly lottery procedure in order to get an admission ticket. For instance, in the year 1995 more than 600 out of about 4,000 applicants had made at least two earlier attempts to be admitted.

–If an applicant is rejected there is an opportunity for appeal. A committee looks into individual cases and has the authority to change the decision. (Goudappel, 1999)

–The actual distribution of the students into the universities is made centrally taking into account the first, second or possibly third preferences of the students. Drenth comments that "For the students in the Netherlands, however, the choice of the university is much less conspicuous than the decision to be allowed to study medicine at all."

The rationale and origins of the 'Dutch system': The 'weighted lottery model' emerged as a compromise in 1972 between two opposite and scarcely reconcilable points of view. On the one hand were the leftist parties and the student representatives. They stressed that according to Dutch legislation everyone who has completed the school-leaving examinations with the proper subjects is entitled to start the academic study of his or her choice. If there are more applicants than available places then the only fair way to implement this entitlement is to decide admissions by the drawing of lots. Drenth tells me (again in correspondence) that the idea of a weighted lottery was suggested in the 1970s by psychologists; he names de Groot and Wiegersma. But it was a Christian Democratic parliamentarian named Vermaat who proposed the idea as well as the actual formula for the weighted lottery that existed from 1975 up to 1998. Vermaat was an economist, who later became a full-time professor of economics at The Vrije Universiteit, Amsterdam (which co-incidentally is Drenth's university).

The opposite point of view was held by the more conservative parties, employers organisations, representatives of the medical profession and, certainly in the beginning, most of the medical faculties. In their view the main entry criterion should be the maximisation of the chances of success on the chosen course of medical study. Applicants should be selected on the basis of variables that predict this success. It was assumed that secondary school achievements would be the best predictor of performance in the medical study. Consequently, it was suggested that the grade point average from the national secondary school final examinations should be the sole basis for selection (and so should *not* include the teachers' assessments).

Neither of these two points of view was able to get the support of a political majority in parliament. One view which appealed to neither group was to introduce rationing by charging. The feeling was that "Education is a public service, not an economic commodity" as Drenth put it. Instead, the weighted lottery model was developed as a compromise; it proved acceptable for both sides in the argument. And so it was that the Netherlands began to chose students for high-demand courses, and for 23 years the Dutch-model weighted lottery system persisted.

Post-allocation trading: (33) Medical Schools, Norway 1989: The system used in the Netherlands may be unusual but it is not unique. Elster (1989), who has written up the Dutch example extensively also records the practice in use in Norway. In an intriguing footnote (p78) Elster, who is Norwegian, notes the custom of 'post-allocative trading' of study opportunities: "Students who are admitted to medical school at Bergen are reported to pay about £2,000 to exchange their place for a similar place in Oslo." Economists of my acquaintance frequently ask about the possibility of post-allocative trading. If it exists, or even if it might be attractive for some of the participants this 'proves' the economists' case that lottery selection is less than (Pareto) optimal. If there is any incentive to trade then a better distribution, better for the customers anyway, can be achieved in this hypothetical market. Any money that might change hands is 'rent', a free gift, usually from the hard-pressed taxpayers. Post-allocative trading is allowed to limited extent in the Dutch system, but through official channels only. Lottery winners who have been offered a place at one university have a small window of opportunity to apply to swap for a similar place at another university. "The chance of a successful trade is small" warns the official website *(www.ib-groep.nl)*.

What do the 'victims' of lottery selection think about it?

Hofstee (1990) who is also Dutch, comments that the adoption of a mixed system of grade scores and a weighted lottery is "apart from a political compromise, may be taken as testimony to the wisdom of the Dutch authorities." Hofstee has also conducted research in the Netherlands into the acceptability of lottery selection compared with other methods. In one study on potential students for advanced medical training he found little enthusiasm for single selection mechanisms. In particular, the use of lotteries as a sole means of selection was highly unacceptable. Instead his respondents expressed a preference for mixed methods which involve educational grades, interviews, waiting lists, psychological tests; in short what Hofstee calls "fuzziness and indeterminacy".

Later a similar questionnaire was administered to 100 Dutch university students of psychology. In contrast to Hofstee's earlier study, these students found a lottery to be a most acceptable mechanism for educational selection. As these were second year students, they, or at least many of their school-mates would have been through such a selection process. Their only exception to the acceptability of lottery selection arises in employment (which as students they may have had little experience of): For promotions and lay-offs these students thought a lottery mechanism would be unacceptable. Hofstee also refers to an earlier study in 1976 (in Scarvia & Helmick 1983) which found that Dutch youngsters preferred a weighted lottery for admission to *numerus fixus* courses with restricted entry rather than either a straight lottery or selection by test scores only. Familiarity with lottery systems seems to produce feelings of acceptability with their use.

1996: the complaint of Meike Vernooij: In operation since 1975, the weighted-lottery mechanism came under intense scrutiny in 1996 when a very bright student called Meike Vernooij[10] was rejected for medical school entry despite gaining near-top grades (9.6 out of 10) in her school-leaving tests. Her case became a national cause célèbre, and resulted in the system being changed. In the process much light was again shed on "the bizarre Dutch weighted-lottery". Meike, it was reported (*THES*, Jul 19, 1996) had wanted to be a doctor ever since she could remember. In her spare time she had been working in the research laboratories of the medical faculty of Erasmus University, Rotterdam. The academics at Erasmus felt that both academically and personally she was well equipped to make an excellent doctor. Impressed by her research work they made no secret of the fact that they wished to guarantee her a place on their course, regardless of the results of the government's weighted lottery procedure.

But Meike had been awarded a high lottery number (5175) which meant she had a very slim chance. In fact she applied no fewer than *three* times. With her score of 9.6 she had an 80% chance of being accepted each time. To be rejected three times was very unlucky. With a 20% chance of being rejected each time, her overall chance of rejection was less than 1% ($0.20^3 = 0.008$).

---

[10] In the newspaper reports from the time her name is mis-spelled as 'Vernooy'

Jo Ritzen, the Minister of Education at the time, immediately questioned the legitimacy of the university's non-standard offer and, according to a ministry spokesman, "was looking into ways of stopping this kind of precedent". Faced with the prospect of legal action, Erasmus dropped its offer to Meike. Frank Munnichs of Erasmus University said: "It's a stupid system. Generally speaking it benefits average quality students rather than bright ones. Also it doesn't take into account other qualities that make a good doctor like good social skills and caring."

Subsequently according to newspaper reports (*Volksrant,* Jul 6, 1996) there was an outcry about this ruling. The father of Meike Vernooij and other school-mates attested to her high motivation. But did she just have a childish infatuation, an affection for science that will cool quickly? If not how will the lottery machine in Groningen know? The move has come as a disappointment to a newly formed group of parents called Lottery Losers, whose children, they claim, are casualties of the lottery system.

Meike Verooij in 2010

Later the story began to develop (*Volksrant,* Jul 10, 1996): In the view of Education Minister Ritzen institutions should not use tricks to circumvent the lottery. But from Maassluis, which is the home-town of the Vernooij family came the comment from Meike's father: "It's a sick system and the Minister should now give a commitment to withdraw his ruling to the University. Ritzen should explain why a student with a score of nine cannot get in automatically." At the same time he wrote a letter to the Lower House, where the injustice of wasting the talents of his daughter was indicated.

The Rotterdam media published his complaint. Then a whole media circus started. A former Minister, Van Kemenade who defended the draw was accused of "living with an ideology two decades out of date, "as if time stands still". Others felt it was time for more interviews with candidates. "The university staff should be willing to speak to all 800 candidates, and not just the official staff but also, why not by flocks of professors? Only then can the motivation be judged to justify why he or she may or may not be offered a place. This discussion was all about the lottery and by the end of it maybe no-one would grieve if it was ended." (*Volksrant*, Jul 10, 1996)

As a result of this 'media circus' the Minister for Education commissioned Professor Drenth to investigate the whole issue. This was despite the fact that according to Ben Wilbrink (in private correspondence) "Everything to be known about the weighted lottery procedure and its costs and benefits, was known already in the seventies." Just as in the UK, a commission of enquiry seems to be the politicians easy method of avoiding taking a difficult decision or of deflecting public outrage. It looks very much like that is what happened in the Netherlands as well.

Drenth who was a professor of psychology at the Free University (Vrije Universiteit) Amsterdam had written previously about selection of students for university. As president of the Royal Academy of Arts and Sciences of the Netherlands (KNAW) he was clearly an establishment figure. In 1995 he had delivered the Duijker Lecture titled: 'Selection of a good student is difficult'. Other papers on the topic included: 'Selection Problems - The assessment of suitability for office, study and occupation' by Prof. Dr. S. 'Admission to the *numerus fixus* again' a discussion by selection expert Mr. B. Wilbrink (1980), or Erasmus' own Prof. Dr. A. who in 1971 wrote an article: 'Some thoughts on the selection for higher medical education'. (All of these papers are in Dutch, of course, with my version of Google translation.) But it is to the Drenth Report and what it reveals about selection using a weighted lottery that I turn in the next section.

Discretion: Another feature of the Dutch system: Before considering the Drenth Report in detail it is worth looking at another feature of the Dutch weighted-lottery system. A small number of cases (5 percent) are dealt with using 'discretion'. This is best illustrated by the case of Karla Bergervoot whose problems with lottery-entry also attracted media attention (Goudappel, 1999). By 1998 she too had lost out in the lottery for the study of medicine three years in a row. Her case did not attract as much attention as Meike Vernooij's because she was finally admitted on grounds of hardship.

The reasons why she was able to secure this exceptional entry related to the fact that Karla had a twin sister. They both lived with their parents. Previously Karla's twin had won the lottery to study medicine on her first attempt. The fact that her twin sister was able to study medicine and that Karla was confronted with this on a daily basis led to psychological problems for Karla, and it influenced both the relationship with her sister and her life as such. The appeal panel decided that both medical social problems made this one of the instances in which losing the lottery could lead to unreasonableness. Thus, a very vague category created by the 'hardship' clause opened the way for some students who have lost out in the lottery.

Meanwhile it may be of interest to know what happened subsequently to Meike Vernooij, for whom discretion was not extended. She was eventually able to study medicine because she became an employee of Erasmus University. Studying medicine was needed as part of her employment. She has since graduated and Dr. Vernooij has worked since June 2002 as a physician-researcher in the department Epidemiology at Erasmus University Medical Centre. She is also in training as a radiologist. And with some success: She is the lead co-author of an article in the prestigious New England Journal of Medicine (Vernooij et al, 2007).

Conclusions of the 'Drenth' Commission: Under political pressure the Dutch minister of education had set up a commission (*Commissie Toealting Numerus Fixus*) chaired by Professor Drenth.

Known as the Drenth Commission, it had examined and evaluated the existing system. Its Report was published in 1997. Broadly speaking it concluded that the existing system was sound and but that it should be modified in some fairly minor ways. The Drenth Report provides a wealth of useful material about an existing lottery-based allocation mechanism which had be in use for decades and had involved thousands of students. The evidence which it collected and presented makes a formidable case for the appropriate use of some form of merit criterion with a weighted lottery being the final arbiter.

How well did the system work? Drenth tested the ability of entry scores to predict performance on the course. At the end of the first level, it was found that entry scores gave some indication of time taken to complete the level, and also the success rate. By the time of the finals, this variation had practically disappeared. The actual results which Drenth presented are shown in graphical form below.

Q1: How well does entry grade predict successful completion?
Drenth produced the following graphs which I reproduce here (in modified form)

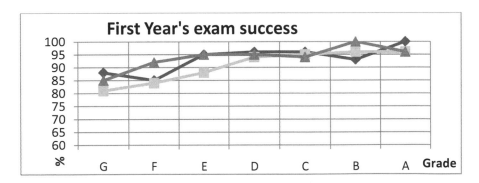

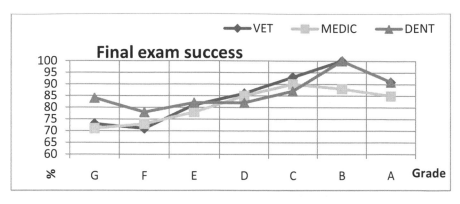

Source: Report of the Drenth Commission, 1997

As Drenth observes, the scores F to A have some predictive validity for academic achievement. This predictive ability works better at the first stage, less so later. But even students in the lowest lottery category F still have about 85% chance to pass the first stage examinations successfully, and more than 70% chance to pass the final qualifying examination eventually.

No matter how well qualified a student is at entry there is always some level of attrition (failure). Even amongst the A-scorers, 5% or 10% still do not get through the course. This means that the entry grade has some, albeit not very strong relationship with the results, according to Drenth (although I think most researchers would be happy to identify significant positive relationships in the data as shown by the graphs above).

Later research by Cohen-Schotanus (2006) on the same theme, found much the same result. Grades on entry can predict how quickly students will complete their course, and how well they will do in their final examinations. In follow-up studies, grades also gave a good prediction of career success as measured by academic publications.

Another more scientific study is reported from Leiden by ten Cate & Hendrix (2009). Starting in 2000, two of the eight Dutch medical schools started selection experiments for 10% of their places. Instead of using the lottery method, some 54 applicants who had volunteered were ranked on the basis of assessments and tests; 24 of them were admitted. The medical schools were reported to be satisfied with the manner in which the selection procedure worked. Did the conventionally chosen students shine in comparison to their randomly picked peers? "it is not yet possible to draw any definite conclusions about the effectiveness of the selection procedure," say ten Cate & Hendrix.

Other researchers are not so reticent: A 'controlled experiment' was carried out at Erasmus University between 2001 and 2004. Some students were chosen by lottery, others were admitted after a selection procedure. According to a team of Dutch researchers (Urlings-Strop et al, 2009) "The main outcome of the selection experiment was that relative risk for dropping out of medical school was 2.6 times lower for selected students than for lottery-admitted controls." Amazingly, and not given the same emphasis was the admission that "Except in the 2001 cohort, there were no significant differences between the percentages of students who performed optimally in either group."

In other words the elaborate selection procedure did no better than the weighted lottery in predicting student achievement. Even the improved drop-out rate may not have been all it seemed: "It seems reasonable to postulate that the outcome of our selection was a product mainly of the procedure, but also, to a certain extent, of self-selection by the applicants themselves, the latter because some applicants were rejected and some withdrew voluntarily throughout the entire course of the selection procedure." In other words, as with previous school lottery studies in Chapter 4, the selection bias may invalidate the main conclusion about dropout rates. Thus the conclusion that the weighted lottery system is just as good as conventional selection procedures at identifying talent has not been invalidated. And of course as well as simplicity, lottery choosing has many other virtues such as avoidance of bias.

Q2 Does entry grade predict time-to-completion rate? Drenth produced these graphics:

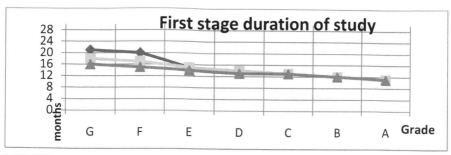

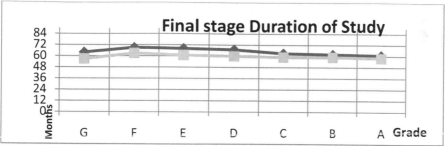

Source: Report of the Drenth Commission, 1997

Although very much stronger at predicting time to complete the first level of the course, entry grade has little effect on time taken over the final stage.

Alternatives to the weighted lottery scheme: Could other methods of selection do better? Drenth also examined alternative entry systems which are used in other countries, especially those related to medical school entry: These include greater use of school-leaving scores, special aptitude tests (such as SATs in the US), psychological tests, interviews, references and the use of probation periods. Apart from school-leaving results, none had much useful predictive power, with interviews and references especially useless.

Returning to the actual weighted lottery, and the results which it achieved in the Netherlands for the three medical courses,

Drenth reminds us that only the top 10% of school leavers are eligible to apply. "Apparently success in the highest stream is a sufficient pre-condition for success on these courses at the university level." The present weighted lottery system, which favours the higher scorers within this group, is characterised, *not* by accepting too many who fail, rather that it rejects too many who would have passed: Returning to the 3,686 students who applied with grades A to F the outcome can be shown as:

WEIGHTED LOTTERY: (What actually happened)

	Accepted	Rejected	Expected Outcome
Total	1,375	2,311	3,686
of whom Pass	1,139	1,852	2,991
and Fail	236	459	695

The scandal (for Drenth) is not that this shows that too many (236 highlighted) candidates have been accepted and then go on to fail. It is that nearly *eight* times as many (1,852) were rejected, yet they would have succeeded.

I will return to this idea of 'balance of risks' when I re-examine the idea of a weighted lottery in the next Chapter. For Drenth this is a clear-cut example of the 'irreconcilables': Firstly considering justice for the applicants: this system throws away the talents of a great many students who have the ability to succeed (although most will be able to apply themselves in other fields). On the other hand, if efficiency considerations predominate in this publicly funded system, more 'product' could be produced. Had the selectors been allowed to pick only those with the highest entry-level scores, then more (about 67 more, I calculate) much-needed health professionals would have passed, not failed. A selection system which always favoured the highest scorers on entry might well produce more product, doctors in this case, than the more egalitarian lottery system. Even so there would still be some who failed.

This also leaves out of account the 'creaming-off' effects – that too many of the best and brightest crowd in to one profession, leaving other equally valuable careers like engineering bereft of talent. Another problem is that of the false challenge – just because a course is difficult to enter, and demands high entry grades, then top performers will apply just because they know they will be accepted. (Economists would call this false signalling).

Drenth's proposals for reform of the weighted lottery system: There were some minor recommendations; that the centralised clearing-house system should be devolved to the medical schools; that candidates should be limited to two applications (as opposed to the unlimited number previously). This last was to encourage those who are not going to gain entry to find some other way of using their talents. Drenth rejected the idea of a simple lottery for all applicants (this would be an example of a 'threshold lottery' not a free-for-all, because places are only open to the top 10% of school-leavers). A simple lottery, Drenth felt would reduce the incentive effects for students to achieve good grades in their school-leaving tests (and produce more failures, a point he did not make).

But it was for the sake of justice that Drenth made his most significant proposal, saying that it was socially unacceptable to reject very high scorers. His proposal was that 50% of places be reserved for the top scorers and 10% are retained for special cases. The remaining 40% would then be awarded by a simple un-weighted lottery.

In response to the Drenth report, the Dutch government decided to stick with the basic system, but modify it somewhat. Top-scoring students (A, B and C) were to be automatically given places. Since generally less than 50% score this highly, this would mean that fewer than the top 50% would gain automatic entry. It would be unfair, according to the legislators to automatically accept someone one year who had a score which previously would not make them automatic winners. Those scoring lower grades would continue to be selected by a weighted lottery, but the weights were altered slightly. Instead of allowing two chances at the lottery, three was the limit. Some de-centralisation of admissions was to be tried out.

Practical politics and the use of lotteries

It is interesting to discover the reasoned deliberations of the Drenth Commission and the response of the Dutch minister of education to the recommendations. In several of the examples in this book the influence of 'practical politics' – the day-to-day reality of the processes rather than the abstract, theoretical models of democracy can be seen. Is there some way of understanding these murky processes, something that would aid those who wish to change the system for the better? What are the mechanics of influencing political processes via voter power, the media, pressure groups, politicians and their advisers?

The Theory of Public Choice, the economists' explanation for the way politicians and others behave has already been encountered (in Chapter 1). This assumes that all the players act solely from their own self-interest. Thus the young lady Meike Vernooij can safely be described as a 'rent-seeker', attempting to capture the free gift of a university place which will lead to higher income later on. Not for her the altruistic acquiescence in the public good of prizes being shared by lottery. The journalists who took up her case might be understood to see a good story involving a clever girl, middle-class and hard-working which would appeal to the readers. The minister of education, as a politician, would seek to maximise the currency of politics which is votes. He might calculate that pandering to the vociferous elite parents would gain votes; the alternative of explaining the democratic nature of weighted lottery selection would not be understood by the public at large, nor would they care very much about it.

Such cynicism about the motives of the players in these processes can only come from those such as economists with a wizened view of humanity as single-mindedly greed-driven. Such gross simplification may lead to some useful conclusions, but ignores the full range of human motivations such as self-esteem and a regard for inter-personal relationships. Rather than pursue a psychological methodology in understanding the impetus behind the adoption of any particular policy, such as a weighted lottery, it might be useful to look at ideas about the dynamics of 'public opinion' in policy formation, or as happened in this case, a change of policy.

There are many general explanations of political ideas such as Barbara Goodwin's 'Using political ideas'(2007). These deal with the theory and the generalised beliefs that underlie political systems like democracies. One feature of democracy is that it should represent the General Will (p313). That still leaves open the question of what this might mean in practice. When it comes to the world of practical politics the picture becomes much murkier. Individuals act out of self-interest (the economists are not entirely wide of the mark), and not necessarily for the greater good. Policy makers may have outdated notions of what needs to be done (Keynes' "slaves to a defunct economist" explanation). But perhaps the most unsavoury aspects of the political process is the machinations of lobbyists and pressure groups.

Some philosophers despair that the system can ever be cleaned up and advocate forms of sortition: This would replace elected representatives by citizens chosen by lottery – see for example Sutherland (2004), Callenbach & Phillips (1985), Barnett & Carthy (1998). A more extreme version called 'Demarchy' by Burnheim (1985) would have all functions of the state devolved to local committees drawn randomly from those involved. I mention these primarily because they involve the use of lotteries, which is a main theme of this book. But these lotteries are about changing the system of politics and I will leave it to its advocates to explain why life would be better with sortition. I am looking at the workings of 'democracy' as it exists, in particular when it involves a proposal to implement, change or abandon some element of lottery in the allocation of school or university places.

As to practical politics on the grand scale, I will leave it to polemicists like Chomsky (1988) to explain, as he does, how consent is manufactured for public approval of such things as 'the war on terror' and most importantly the spending of huge amounts of tax-payers money. This process is driven by well-financed lobbyists acting for powerful vested interests. Public opinion will be moulded by the media in the interests of those with influence. All of this is well-known, but hardly applies to the more mundane business of altering the admissions arrangements for state-funded schools or universities.

A very interesting exploratory study was carried out by Susan Herbst (1998) on the factors which affect the political process in these more humdrum decisions, such as school-places by lottery or not. She draws on the model of 'protective democracy' proposed by David Held. In this form of democracy the government protects individuals from others, and enables them to pursue their own interests. Central to making this form of democracy work involves gauging public opinion and understanding what it is. Herbst's real-life investigations with elected politicians and their advisors (generally referred to as 'staffers' in the US context) as well as political journalists gives a different and in many ways more realistic view of the political process. What she discovered was a thoughtful wish to seek out public opinion and to implement it. This corresponded to what she called a 'folk model' or 'lay theory' of what democracy entailed.

What this 'public opinion' was and how it was to be discovered was not what might be expected. Clearly the modern science of public opinion polling would have some impact, but polls are expensive and not always relevant. "Polling will not tell us whether people will act on their opinions." (p153) Journalists she found are 'startled' by the degree of ignorance shown by their readership, which throws into doubt the value of opinions given in opinion polls.

So 'public opinion' becomes a social construct, to use sociological jargon. The professionals use various means to assess it: They may use local means to test intensity of feeling. Lobbyists will provide information; it may be partial information, but unless it is reliable lobbyists lose their reputation. Perhaps most surprisingly, professionals rely on news media for reports of 'public opinion'.

Returning to the saga of Meike Vernooij and the changes to the Netherlands medical school weighted lottery entry system we can interpret the behaviour of the actors in a more realistic and less mean-spirited manner. There are no powerful well-funded lobbies seeking to extract 'rent' from the taxpayer. Corporate bodies like the medical associations and the university lecturers' trade union have influence, but their advice will (mostly) be intended to promote the general good, not enrich their members. The minister of education who made the fateful decision to firstly set up the Drenth commission, and then partly rejected its recommendations was acting at least in part with the same benevolent intentions, although vote-catching would also have played a part. As for Miss Vernooij herself, calling in aid notions of fairness and merit was, in these circumstances, self-interested, but could work against her at other times. The students' union which had always been a staunch supporter of the weighted lottery could still be accused of wanting to give their members an easy ride, but did so for entirely defensible reasons.

So too, in the earlier example of the formation of the English Schools Admissions Code, we can see higher motives at work. The (mostly Labour) politicians who drafted the code may have been motivated by class-envy, seeing the better-off buying themselves places at good schools because they could afford the houses in the better catchment areas. But that was secondary to the wish to spread equality of opportunity more widely. In this they were informed by journalistic endeavours as well as the work of independent think-tanks like the Social Market Foundation. (I have previously remarked on this rare glimpse of government policy being shaped by an outside lobbying institute.) They were determined to press ahead with a lottery despite the obvious negative reaction they must have known would be found amongst the public. It was only later that the Sutton Trust discovered that public opinion could get to like lottery selection if the proposition was framed in an appropriate way.

However, this satisfaction with the courage of politicians to insist on what they believed was right even if it did not seem to be popular may not survive the more robust tests of public opinion. Ministers of education both in 1994 and again in 2009 as we saw (Lancashire, English Code follow-up) have been quick to shoot off 'sound-bite' rejections of the use of lotteries, preferring to hide behind the judgements of the courts or of the Schools Adjudicator.

Herbst drew her conclusions on the basis of a study amongst legislators in the US state of Illinois (which includes the city of Chicago). Of course one controversy they would not have to deal with is using lotteries to distribute school places. A wide consensus seems to exist in support of lotteries both from the opinion formers and the public at large. No opinion polls support this view, apart from the single dubious negative poll in Carnavale & Rose (2003); it just seems to be a settled part of the democratic landscape.

Herbst also pointed out that what was taken to be 'public opinion' depended on both a shared model of democracy and the technology for the assessment of opinion. The fundamentals of elective democracy have been challenged in the past with calls for more participation with calls for citizens juries to review policies. More recently advocates of sortition, which would give us politicians by lottery, have become more vocal. The technology for imposing opinions through the media has been greatly weakened by the rise of the internet, as have the possibilities for measuring the strength of opinions. The practicalities of policy formation for issues like school admissions may look quite different in years to come, and one might hope will better reflect the general will.

Chapter 9

Lotteries for University Places: Dubious or Efficient & Fair?

In the conclusion to his densely argued 1999 book *On lotteries and legal decision-making* Neil Duxbury felt (p 175) that he had turned "a ludicrous idea into a dubious one." You may still feel that using lotteries to decide places at university to be dubious at best. It would indeed be ludicrous to say that university places should be open to all whatever their talents or abilities. Universities *must* select on academic grounds. The idea that a randomisation mechanism could be the sole decider of who wins a place would be quite improper, and flies in the face of the need for a test of academic achievement. So what, if anything, can justify using a lottery as part of the selection process for university students?

Lotteries may be practical and convenient, for example when deciding which borderline candidates to accept. Lotteries, it is claimed (Stone, 2010) may have the virtues of "impartiality", "honesty", "unbiased-ness" even "sanitisation". These important, but somewhat abstract virtues can be difficult to pin down. I will stick with the more tractable attributes of *efficiency* and *fairness*, testing the use of lotteries for university places against these two. For both I will try to avoid abstraction and seek instead practical measurable parameters to test both simple lotteries like the Irish borderline grades example (27), as well as the highly controversial Netherlands weighted lottery system (32) against these criteria.

Previously (in Chapter 7) I introduced the idea of Meritocracy, because 'merit' is generally accepted as the best and fairest means of selecting students for university and college courses. Since there is little agreement on what, objectively, merit actually means I tackled two aspects of this. Firstly on the use of interviews, I showed on the basis of the evidence, interviews are pretty well useless for identifying 'merit', mere noise in the system, or a decorous ceremony. Secondly taking 'good works' into account leaves the process wide open to discrimination of all kinds. These are the 'bad' reasons which the use of a lottery would preclude.

In this chapter I will argue against what seems to be a much less contentious interpretation of selection on merit – that of always preferring the top-scoring candidate. This may be a sensible strategy for the particular course at a university or college, but it will be unfair to many of those applying. Common-sense suggests that deliberately choosing less well pre-qualified applicants would be a recipe for lower levels of achievement on the course. It seems grossly unfair that applicants who had worked hard to obtain top entry grades should be passed over in favour of lesser-qualified entrants. Yet this is the commonsense which I intend to challenge, drawing especially on the evidence from the Netherlands experience as reported by Drenth. Because of the use of random selection this provides a rare example of scientifically validated experimental data and is therefore a sound basis for drawing conclusions.

In this chapter I will look first at 'efficiency' as applied to using scores in the selection process and how far these scores can provide an indicator of future success. Then I will tackle 'fairness' in a systematic way, like an engineer, using the analogy of the well-developed industrial procedures used in quality control. From this I hope to show that the Dutch example is both fair and efficient, and indeed, as Drenth himself indicated could be extended. Weighted lotteries could be the justifiable form of selection which recognises valid merit and is yet both efficient and fair.

Efficiency in academic selection:

The most efficient selection process would seem to be the one which identifies those candidates who have the highest chance of succeeding on whatever course they are being selected for. Locally, for that particular course this makes sense. But this is just one course amongst many in the educational system. Globally, when all the players in the system are considered, efficiency may not be represented by the simplistic strategy of individual courses always picking the highest scorers.

What difference would it make if a university course adopted a policy of always preferring the top scorers at entry? Returning to the figures given by Drenth, where students had been selected by a weighted lottery, the results were as follows:

WEIGHTED LOTTERY: (What actually happened)

	Accepted	Rejected	Expected Outcome
Total	1,375	2,311	3,686
of whom Pass	1,139	1,852	2,991
and Fail	236	459	695

Because of the weighted lottery not all of the 'Accepted' are from the top scorers available. Has the lottery allowed too many duds to sneak in? If so could the selection system be improved for this course so that there are fewer failures?

If the university course could cherry-pick, and only accept the top scoring applicants this would be the result: (The calculations are based on the figures given by Drenth.)

CHERRY-PICKING: (Only pick top-scorers)

	Accepted	Rejected	Expected Outcome
Total	1,375	2,311	3,686
Pass	1,206	1,785	2,991
Fail	169	526	695

In this second hypothetical scenario there are 67 more professionals produced (1206 compared to 1139) which is a 5% improvement in medical school productivity. If these establishments are to be viewed as factories producing professionals the answer is clear-cut: Always choose the top-scorers on entry, because that will deliver most product.

I think most readers would re-act with distaste at this mechanistic philosophy. Grand notions of education being a public service not an industry may be all well and good, but public money is being spent here. Are we to tell the taxpayers to spend more so that a few students can try their hand at their chosen course, and then fail? Or that if 5% more medical professionals are deemed to be needed then space at medical schools must be expanded (and paid for). Put like this the answer is not difficult to work out.

Difficulties with systematically choosing the top scorers on entry: This simple mechanism suffers from some significant measurement difficulties in identifying who will do best on a given course. Although it remains the case that higher scorers can generally be expected to do better, this prediction is very 'noisy'. A study by Bekhrandia (2002) looked at an entire student cohort. He again discovered the trend: that better entry scores predict better final degree grades *on average*. But it is clear that there is a lot of unpredictability in the system: an entrant with 18 points (UK A-levels) still has a 60% chance of doing as well or better than an entrant with 24 points. (This of course reinforces the fuzzy nature of performance as predicted by entry scores which was highlighted in Chapter 7.)

Entry tests have been shown to give misleading results when race or class is taken into account. Bekhrandia (2003) produces evidence to show that pupils from the state sector do much better than those from independent (fee-paying) schools for the same A-level entry points. Independent school pupils have been intensively coached to gain better A-levels but would need to gain an extra four A-level points to have the same expected degree.

Entry criteria could be made more efficient if we could only cast aside our liberal prejudices. If the additional factors of race and gender were allowed to be factored in, then better results could be obtained through discrimination. For example, it has been shown (Ferguson et al, 2002) that white women can be expected to perform better on medical courses than men or ethnic minority students. Following the logic of the hypothetical example above, then the rule should always be: "Choose the top-scoring white females". But no, of course such a rule is unacceptable, struck out on discriminatory grounds. Mere local efficiency is over-ruled by global fairness in this case.

When higher scores do not indicate better performance: There are two features in the relationship between scores on entry and future performance which undermine the simplistic notion that highest scores always do best. These two features emanate from the *uncertainty* and *non-linearity* which are inevitable when using test scores. I have already explained how there is a great deal of uncertainty in the relationship between entry scores and final degree results. But there is another feature which makes the use of entry scores even more suspect as the sole arbiter of entry to university because 'higher grades predict greater success'. Research has shown that the relationship between scores and predicted performance may become almost meaningless once the scores on entry have attained a certain level. A hint of this was given in example (29) when entry to nursing courses was open to all who had scored C-grade or better, on the (researched) grounds that there was no evidence that those with higher entry scores did any better.

Non-linearity: more is not always better: The common-sense notion is that the score on an IQ test or entry level grades is, grade for grade always a sound indicator of future academic performance. In many cases this is not so. Often the predicted performance may generally rise with IQ score, but beyond some (surprisingly low) point then tends to level off.

There are many examples in the literature of entry tests or scores showing a linear, if fuzzy relationship up to a certain level, then flattening out after that. Here are a few that I have found:

– Pilot training: War time pilot training, like much research based on large-scale military activity, shows this non-linear characteristic. Eysenck (1962) reported with a simple graphic (p26) that pilot performance generally increased in line with IQ, but beyond a score of 120 there is scarcely any improvement.

– University entrance NL: In the Netherlands Drenth (1999) described the performance of medical students as predicted by their entry grades. Because of the natural experiment provided by random selection, a representative cross-section of eligible students with a range of grades are accepted onto the courses. Drenth concludes that achievement in final secondary school examinations "does have some, although not very strong, relationship with the study results in the medical studies, especially in the early years (of the course) and if time criteria (time taken to complete) are used. Other predictors have negligible correlations." Drenth also points out that those in the lowest category for entry qualifications still have a good chance to succeed and finish their studies in a reasonable time.

– University entrance UK: Having explained that there is a strong (0.50) correlation between measured IQ and academic performance, Kline (1991) states quite bluntly: (p9) "if our sample is selected for intelligence (for example at a good university where all students have IQs beyond 120) then the correlation is bound to fail. Everyone has sufficient ability to do the work." This view is supported by two more recent reports which asked how well A-levels predict final degree classification: Wiliam (*BBC News*, Aug 13, 2002) studied the results of students graduating from his own institution, King's College. Wiliam concluded that using A-level points to predict class of degree is only slightly better than pure chance. (Since this is an elite university, then this result is in line with what Drenth found in the Netherlands).

Taken together, these findings point to the wisdom of Glendale nursing (29) using a cut-off score of C-grade for entry, and conducting a lottery for the survivors. The flat part of the relationship suggests too, that when elite courses are choosing from highly qualified applicants there is very little to be gained by going for the highest scorers. All applicants in this case have shown sufficient achievement to succeed.

Wider reasons for not seeking local efficiency through maximising entry scores: Global efficiency: It may be efficient in a narrow, local sense if a particular course in a university always selects the top-scorers. The taxpayer may seem to be receiving slightly better value for money by this. But efficiency can be seen in a broader context:

For the applicant cohort, the effort put in to achieving their high, but not quite high enough scores may represent a waste. I know of many students who have repeated a year at school in order to achieve higher grades. This did not make them innately cleverer, but it certainly wasted their time. To get some idea of the waste I conducted a small investigation at Swansea University on first year Economics students (Boyle, 2006). I discovered that about one quarter of them had spent time gaining extra grade-points. Each repeater had spent on average four months of his or her life to achieve this. This is a clear example of wasted effort devoted to 'rent-seeking' as the economists call it.

Another reason for rejecting the 'highest entry scorer always wins' admission criterion is more nebulous. Such schemes will crowd-in the best and brightest onto courses at the most prestigious establishments – what might be called the 'Oxbridge effect'. Doing so deprives less prestigious courses and universities of these talents. Had the top-scorers been spread around more there may have been a general uplift to achievement generally. That could be efficient for society as a whole if such mixing of students with different abilities raises achievement overall. This 'peer-group effect' is borne out by evidence drawn from the use of lottery-allocation, as will be seen in the next chapter.

Another similar reason for deviating from the 'highest scorers always win' entry criterion might be the value of diversity. A case could be made for choosing students from different (but always adequate) levels of achievement. Education is a good which is consumed collectively by groups coming together to study in lectures, seminars and tutorials. Only rarely do students complete a degree course entirely alone. One of the benefits of university learning may come from a good social mixture in the student body. The slight inefficiency of admitting less-well pre-qualified (but always adequately qualified) candidates for the sake of diversity in the student group has to be balanced against the improved performance of the group, usually in ways which are not measured. Gains in social skills may be all-important for medical professionals, for example, but they are difficult to measure.

Another 'social production' argument has arisen specifically in the case of medical practitioners. For decades medical schools have attracted the elite students. This is great for the future supply of highly qualified specialists but creates problems further down the line. The practice of medicine also requires family doctors, less glamorous than brain surgery but vital for the health service. It has not always been easy, nor do the products of medical school find it congenial to accept these less intellectually demanding roles. A more diverse intake would help.

In the same 'general good' theme, it may also be inefficient for society as a whole if many of the best and brightest crowd into medical professions at the expense of, say, science and engineering. Again a more academically diverse entry to the high-demand professional courses may lead to a better national economic performance overall. Diverting some of the best talents into less prestigious careers might raise effectiveness all round.

If efficiency on a single course is the sole yardstick then all of these reasons for deviating from the simple pick the highest scorers rule are difficult to sustain. But if the efficiency of the education system as a whole is considered and when the efforts of the students being processed through it are taken into account then a good case can be made for some form of weighted lottery entry.

Fairness:

If the idea of 'efficiency' is well-defined and agreed, the same cannot be said of 'fairness'. This is not because fairness is not widely invoked. How often has the cry "It's not fair!" gone up from those who have lost out, for example the child who lives next door to a school and yet is not allowed to attend because of a lottery. There may be an intuitive understanding of what constitutes 'fairness' in the population at large, but philosophers and others struggle to produce a simple measurable definition, or avoid defining it altogether, despite frequently using the term.

Take for example the hugely respected John Rawls, in his oft quoted *A Theory of Justice* (1972). He is quite explicit about what fairness means: Chapter 1 is entitled: "Justice as Fairness", but one searches in vain for any definition of either. Economists too, call on 'fairness'; for example Baumol's 1986 book *Superfairness*. (It amounts to little more than allowing free market forces to reign supreme). Statisticians use the concept but in a narrow sense. A 'fair' coin is one which will predictably land heads up 50% of the time. (Curiosity about extending the clear-cut statistical concept of fairness to other affairs was one of my motivations for venturing into the realms of lottery allocation). But for the philosophers there is a noticeable reluctance to define exactly what they mean by fairness.

If the lottery is the epitome of 'fairness' then perhaps the best thing to do is abolish the quest for 'merit' altogether. When large numbers of minimally qualified students apply for a place on a course accept them all, or if numbers must be limited use a lottery. Some such as Astin (1969 and 1970) take the partial failure of tests to reliably predict degree results as a good enough reason, in fairness, to do away with selection altogether. Goldstein made a similar comment on an earlier paper of mine (Boyle, 1998). In the same vein when the shortcomings and unreliability of IQ tests were exposed the conclusion was that they should be abolished.

This is too extreme. Some form of screening of entrants is rational, and one might add it would be very unfair not to apply validated knowledge about selection of entrants for academic courses. But how is such fairness to be decided? In the absence of an agreed definition, I propose, first, the following simple description of fairness which is related to our current concerns, and which could be operationalised as:

> *Fairness means treating as equal all with equal merit.*

This is a simple enough formulation. It would explain the *un-fairness* when Drenth proposed that 50% of places be reserved for top-scoring students. This was over-ruled because it would result in inter-year unfairness. If a score of 7.5 was enough for automatic entry one year then it would be *unfair* between one year and another if the threshold went up to 8.0 the following year, just to maintain the 50% quota.

A similar case could be made for entry to UK medical schools: If the middle-aged doctor who treats you today was accepted with a BBC grade, then it is inter-generationally *unfair* to require AAA today. (I leave out of account the oft stated view that A-levels are getting easier, and assume they are equivalent). These are the incompatibles: efficiency says "always choose the top scorers", fairness says "don't arbitrarily raise the threshold". If a fixed cut-off score produces more applicants than places then in fairness there should be a lottery for those who make the cut.

As well as inter-temporal fairness I would like to make the case for the use of *relevant merit* as opposed to maximum or universal merit. When choosing entrants for an academic course, only valid academic indicators should be used. This probably means a threshold score. Although gaining scores above the threshold represents some form of merit, it would be *unfair* for purposes of selection to require such higher scores. Similarly, since no valid case can be made for their efficacy, it would be *unfair* because of irrelevancy to make use of interviews or to inspect the Good Works undertaken by the candidate. If there is still a surplus of applicants with adequate prior grades then in fairness it is difficult to envisage any alternative, defensible method of selecting apart from a lottery.

Balance of Risks

Previously I suggested a simple definition of Fairness. I would now like to augment this definition of fairness in one small way:

> *Fairness means treating as equal*
> *all those who are **not significantly** different*

I am using 'significantly' in the familiar statistical sense. There is always uncertainty in the measurement of entry scores. This results in predictions of success which are subject to bands of uncertainty. When the university selects students, it has the ability to maximise the benefits for itself. It can do this by minimising the risk of accepting a 'dud' – a student who will fail on the course – by always choosing top-scorers. The risk to the customer, the student who wishes to attend ('purchase') the course is greater. Even by working hard and having invested time and effort into becoming well-enough qualified for the course there is still a high chance of being rejected. So what, you might say; it has always been like this. The powerful will always shed their risks onto those unable to resist this risk-shedding. (A situation which economists have identified in sub-contracting and out-sourcing by large firms, particularly in the construction industry. See for example Ball (1988))

But what if the system was designed so that both parties shared the risk in equal proportions? Can a selection procedure be designed which means that the risk of a student being rejected, even though adequately qualified is equivalent to the risk for the course of accepting a student who will subsequently go on to fail? This may all sound both complex and idealistic, so I will draw on an example from the field of Industrial Statistical Quality Control.

How balancing the risks operates in industry: Acceptance sampling: An example of a situation which balances the risks can be found is industrial statistical schemes of Acceptance Sampling which are applied to incoming supplies. It originated with military production, so the balance of power between the US government and say, the Boeing corporation can be easily understood.

In Acceptance Sampling, the Supplier delivers batch of widgets; the Customer wants to know if they are OK. He may test a few by means of a random sample, and if he finds a faulty widget does he rejects the entire delivery? No! It must be decided in advance what level of reliability is acceptable. Next the way in which the sampling scheme works has to be agreed. The size of the sample, and what action to take depending on how many rejects are found has to be calculated. This results in the 'Operating Characteristic' of the scheme which is usually shown as a graph. I am glossing over a great deal of detail here. There is plenty of information about these matters which can be found on-line and in books such as Montgomery's (2008 6e) *Introduction to Statistical Quality Control*. The subject matter is also enshrined in International Standard ISO 14560: 2004

What makes the industrial practice of acceptance sampling relevant is the way it deals with risk. In any control scheme there are *two* main risks of making a mistake. The batch supplied may be Good, but because of sampling variability it may be recorded as Reject. The other risk is that the batch is Bad, but may be let through as Good. (More statistically literate readers will recognise the Type I and Type II errors here). Either form of mistake produces an undesirable result, and could impact negatively on either supplier or customer. This is where the balanced compromise comes into play. The risks for both parties are equalised. It is *not* acceptable to place extra risk on one side. This balance of risks is only possible because of the bargaining power of the parties involved.

Returning to more familiar territory of acceptance or rejection of applicants for places on a university course we can look again at the statistics given by Drenth relating to the NL Medical School entry. Pass rates for students increased with their entry score. The top entry scorers with As had a 90% predicted chance of passing; in the same scheme even the lowest scorers at entry had an 75% chance. This is not a balance-of-risks situation. Only the top 10% of school-leavers can apply, so not surprisingly even the worst has a very high chance of passing, if admitted. Remember too, how the weighted lottery worked: the higher your entry score the more likely you would win in the lottery with values ranging from four-fifths for the A-grades down to two-fifths for the lowest F-grades.

Adding in some of the remaining 90% of the cohort will produce applicants with diminishing chances of passing. Given the non-linearity of the relationship between entry grades and chance of passing, maybe only the top one-third of students would have at least a 50% chance of passing. How far down the scale this 50% point happens could be found as a result of researches into the figures.

If there is to be a balance of risks between applicants and the university, then the cut-off point has to be set at the 50% point. If a student has a 50% or greater chance of passing he or she ought to be considered; less than that leads to outright rejection. Of course with a weighted lottery system candidates with only a 50% chance of passing would then have a very *low* chance of actually gaining admission, but not *no chance* as at present. I would describe the present Dutch system as systematically unfair because it only considers the top 10% of school-leavers. I am sure that there are many students in the next 10% of high scorers with at least a 50% chance of success.

Drawing on the model of industrial statistical acceptance sampling gives, I believe, the ultimate in fairness for a selection scheme. It may sound idealistic, but it is worth remembering that that balancing the risks is seen as the proper way to do things in industry. Loading the risks onto the weaker parties (as with most elite university selection) may make practical sense for the university, but it is far from fair.

I have only outlined a possible model of 'ultimate fairness'. There is a similar discussion in an earlier paper by Hofstee (1983). Although he does not refer to industrial techniques, he produces a cross-over graph similar to the operating characteristic which can be found in Acceptance Sampling. He also provides a theoretical framework the calculation of the cut-off point – the minimum score necessary before applicants can enter the weighted lottery. His approach is from a different field but the resultant proposals show marked similarities.

Extending choice and opportunity to those who have a realistic (at least 50%) chance of succeeding would be fair, both to students applying and the university selecting. It would recognise that in a democratic society there should be equal risks for all parties. The practice of the powerful parties in off-loading risks onto the powerless violates this principle. If institutions are not prepared to deal with their clients in such an even-handed way, then legislation to ensure this seems reasonable.

Conclusion on fairness: Courses and universities which demand high entry scores present a challenge and a perverse incentive: just because veterinary courses have the highest entry requirements this may encourage those who are unsuited, but high scoring, to apply. If at first you don't succeed, with a highest-scorer-wins system there is a temptation to repeat a year at school in order to gain higher entry grades. It is difficult to see what educational advantage flows from this wasteful rent-seeking

In my scheme higher grades would not guarantee a place, they would only improve your chances of entry onto a course. This might mean less incentive to gain high grades, leading to an apparent decline in standards. Perhaps an education less targeted on entry grades might well produce more rounded individuals. An even more desirable outcome might be a spreading-out of applicants onto different courses and universities. With no certainty, only a good chance of entry to a prestigious university or a popular course, applicants might re-consider what they really want to do. Choices of vocational course could be based on aptitude for that course, not the entry requirements.

Is it too much to hope that a balanced and fairly weighted lottery entry system could spread out applicants to universities and courses so that supply and demand could be brought more into line with each other? Eventually we might see, like some of the school-entry lotteries that were explained earlier, that the need for a lottery would largely wither away in actual use, but its power could be held in reserve should the bad old ways of selection by highest grades creep in again.

Part III:
Lotteries for
Students and Teachers

Chapter 10

Student Housing in the USA: Strategic Behaviour

Once you have bagged a place at the university of your choice (or maybe it was chosen for you by a lottery!) the next thing to worry about is where to live. This chapter is concerned with the accommodation that can be quite a significant aspect of the educational experience. In the UK we talk of student 'Halls of Residence'; in the US it is 'student housing'. They are both much the same type of purpose-built, university-owned buildings, often on campus. They are rented to students as a place to live while attending a course. At US universities there is a widespread and unusual practice of allocating student housing by means of a lottery. This is rare elsewhere.

This random assignment of places for student housing is of some interest, but mostly I include it because it has provided academics with yet more 'natural experiments'. At the end of this chapter I will look at three areas which have been studied with the aid of this windfall of scientifically validated information. These are: the stability of consumer preferences over time; the effect of peer groups on academic performance, and strategic behaviour of subjects (students) when faced with limited choice mediated by a lottery.

Allocating housing, especially social housing, using a lottery is nothing exceptional. Almost by definition social housing is rented out or sold at less than the market price, so excess demand has to be managed. This is usually by some form of merit system, such as time on a waiting list, or personal circumstances like lone parenthood or disability. Lotteries have sometimes been used, as the following examples show:–

– After the 2004 Olympic Games in Athens there was a lottery for the chance to buy one of the 2,292 apartments used by the athletes. The price was about half the market rate. Only those on low incomes were eligible to take part, low-income being defined as earning less than the national average wage. More than 17,000 eligible Greeks entered. (*BBC News*, Oct 7, 2004)

– In Boston, Massachusetts, applicants for social housing go on a waiting list. All applicants start afresh each year, but a priority waiting list is established using "a computerized random lottery selection process to establish the placement". (*www.bostonhousing.org*, 2008)

– In Hong Kong the Housing Authority periodically conducts an allocation exercise of its housing stock. Flats from several different housing estates are made available and applicants indicate their preferred choice of up to four estates. Successful applicants are drawn by random lottery. The final selection of flats does not depend on the original preferences as stated on the application forms. (Suen & Tang 1984)

US student housing lotteries

To transfer this social-housing mechanism of lottery allocation across to the considerably more privileged field of student housing seems odd, but it certainly happens. Its use is mainly confined to the US and Canada, although I have found one or two UK examples. Lottery use implies giving something away at below market price, which is something which needs investigating, or at least explaining.

(Note: In this section where specific universities are mentioned, I will not give a reference to a website; up-to-date information can easily be found by entering *.edu '*' being the university name or its initials; so *harvard.edu*. Search on 'lottery' and you will soon find the details for that university of their student housing allocation policy)

(34) Student housing in the US: Enter 'university housing lottery' into Google and you will find a torrent of results. In a Google search (Mar 18, 2009) on these keywords I found 297,000 results which had all three words. On the first three pages I found examples of lottery-based student housing allocation at universities such as:

Stanford, Pacific-Oregon, Rowan-New Jersey, Clark-Massachusetts, South east-Missouri, West Florida, Quincy-Illinois, Butler, Scranton, Furman, Brown, Dennison, Connecticut, New Hampshire, Actors New School NY, Binghampton, De Pauw, Dayton, John Hopkins, Wesleyan-Illinois, San Jose, Harvard, Tufts. (all of these are in the USA)

As a further check I looked at an arbitrary set of specific locations – Seattle, Spokane, Denver and Salt Lake City, which I intended to visit shortly. Again, in all four cities I found that universities are using a lottery as part of their student housing allocation process.

From this it seems clear that using a lottery to allocate student housing is very widely used in American universities. A similar search restricted to Canada found a few examples (Guelph-Humber, Queen's Ontario, Victoria), but only after extensive searching. Neither Australia nor the UK produced any results (apart from a lone British example of LSE post-graduate students). So the use of a lottery in student housing allocations is, it seems, largely confined to North America, especially the United States. The description 'lottery' is generally used, although some instances of 'random selection' can be found, for example at Vanderbilt. Elsewhere the rather more coy 'ballot' is preferred.

How lotteries are used: This widespread and repeated use of lotteries in allocating student accommodation at US universities takes many forms:

(a) Simple lotteries: At its simplest the lottery has little impact.

(34a) Chicago allocates rooms on a daily basis effectively on a first-come-first-served basis. However all applications received on a given day are shuffled randomly and dealt with accordingly.

(b) Dictatorial lotteries: Most colleges and universities operate on a yearly cycle, which results in all their student housing being allocated in a single sweep. When doing this some university authorities act in a dictatorial way, ignoring student preferences and scattering students at random throughout their housing. In this system, if rooms are shared then room-mates too are picked at random. Here are some examples of dictatorial lotteries:

(34b) Dartmouth, New Hampshire student housing 2000: Bruce Sacerdote (2000) of Dartmouth College, New Hampshire described such a system which was in use at his university in 2000, having been established in 1994. Dartmouth freshmen are assigned to dorms and roommates randomly. Each freshman fills out and mails in a brief housing slip with answers to four yes/no questions about personal behaviour (smoking, music, late hours and tidiness) plus gender. The slips are then put into 32 piles depending on the answers. The piles are then thoroughly shuffled by hand, and the assignment process begins. There will be more about this example later, because Sacerdote used it to test the peer-group hypothesis: that your room-mate can affect your academic performance for good or ill. Currently Dartmouth operates a more 'customer-friendly' room draw (see below (34e)).

(34c) Harvard student housing 2009: Harvard University also adopts a dictatorial allocation technique, but at the house rather than room level:

> a simple mathematical process will be used to randomly assign individuals, or blocking groups of up to eight freshmen, to the 12 residential Houses. The only control in the lottery is for gender balance.

(34d) Duke student housing 2009: Students are told of their assignment and the fact that it is done at random. A defence and encouragement to participate in this dictatorial system is given by Duke University as:

First-year student housing assignments are done on a random basis. Duke University is committed to encouraging our students to embrace new experiences, and our random process allows students to be exposed to a myriad of cultures, view-points, and value systems.

(c) Place in the queue (line) for housing decided by lottery:

(34e) Dartmouth, New Hampshire student housing 2009: Unlike the previous dictatorial system, the currently (2009) Dartmouth allows students to pick the best available room. Students are randomly assigned a 'priority number' ahead of the allocation process. They then must attend the allocation process on their designated day and time, forming a queue in the order of their assigned priority number. As each person in the queue is processed, they have a free choice over any of the remaining unallocated rooms. So although it is called a 'room draw' this is in fact a draw for priority in a queue (line) where choices can be made from the best available remaining rooms. The most obvious feature of this form of allocation is that it requires students to turn up in person on the day (although proxies may be allowed).

Lottery used to influence student behaviour (34f) Swarthmore 2009: Swarthmore allocates priority in the queue for housing, but with an added twist. Students are warned that:

> A student's individual lottery priority number is affected by discipline points. Each time a student is found responsible for violating a policy, demerits are assigned to the student. The demerits are then used in creating the student's lottery priority number. The lower the lottery number the better. Consequently, every demerit number increases the lottery priority number, giving the student a less desirable lottery number.

Using the lottery to enhance the effectiveness of punishments has been explored elsewhere (Perry et al, 2001). The theory seems to be that if the threat of a fine is an incentive for good behaviour, then the threat of a fine which varies randomly from mild to severe can enhance the incentive effect. It would be interesting to see if Swarthmore's scheme produces better behaviour.

Giving students a random number which translates into priority in choosing accommodation currently seems to be the dominant form of US student housing lottery. This preserves the idea of choice, while sharing the opportunity of exercising that choice at random via a lottery. Randomisation is generally achieved electronically within a mysterious computer operated by the university authorities.

(35) Car parking space lottery, Harvard 2004 I cannot leave this section without a mention of the Harvard car-parking place lottery. Because of the shortage of car-parking at Harvard, the space is rationed. Students who win university parking spaces pay between $90 and $135 per month, far less than they would pay for off-street parking in the City of Cambridge, Mass. (p165 Fox, 2004). The merits of providing subsidised car-parking to students is somewhat difficult to comprehend!

Why use a lottery to allocate student housing?

The rationale for using this particular form of lottery allocation is seldom stated. This may be because of the widely held view in the US that a lottery is such a normal and obvious method to use that it does not need to be explained or defended. One rare defence of the policy comes from Assumption University which states

> The lottery, which was designed many years ago with help from the Student Government Association, is a very <u>fair</u> way of determining housing assignments. No one gets special privilege, except with regard to their class standing (Senior, Junior, Sophomore). .... participating in the random process is a truly educational and eye-opening experience!

Again, as with school-place lotteries, this lack of interest in the US is difficult to understand. The academics are well aware of housing lotteries, and as will be seen later in this chapter, they have used them to develop theories about peer-group effects and strategic behaviour. But no academic, not even an economist seems to have questioned the basic tenet of the lottery, which essentially involves giving away a product (accommodation) at less than the market rate. To put it another way: What is the point of subsidising student housing? The only critique of this that I could find came from a student Colin Marshall (*dailynexus.com*, Aug 28, 2005) at UCSB (where it seems that car parking too, is subject to a lottery):

> **Housing Lottery Lacks Economic Sagacity**: The demand for something outstrips the supply of that thing. Do you (a) let the price rise to an equilibrium where the number of willing buyers equals the number of products, or (b) throw everyone's name into a Soviet-style lottery[11] and hope for the best?......
>
> In the name of so-called equality and fairness, the lotteries are keeping resources away from those who value them most, an odd consequence to allow in an institution where economics is taught. Nevertheless, irrational disdain of the rich and wrongheaded egalitarianism appear to be the orders of the day.

As this highly perceptive student puts it, in terms of theoretical economics it is very hard to justify lottery allocation for student housing or parking. Yet these lotteries are widely used. Perhaps there are other reasons besides the economists' ones which make sense? There is considerable scope for a research project in this field!

Reactions of student-customers to housing lotteries:

The following are some headlines and quotes from student magazines, which may tend to sensationalise what students really think about housing lotteries:

At **Quinnipiac** (*quchronicle.com, Apr 9, 2009)* the story was: "Housing lottery is 'grossly flawed' and leaves us out in the cold with no idea where and who they will be living with next year. The lottery idea is good in theory, but then again so is a Utopia." The grumble here was with the university which had promised to provide accommodation for all, but had failed to explain that some

---

[11] I have never encountered a Soviet-era lottery, although there have been a few post-communist era lotteries to distribute jobs, redundancies and property. See my website *www.conallboyle.com* for examples.

of it was off-campus. Who got to be on or off was to be decided by lottery.

Boston College (*bcheights.com*, Feb 18, 2002) provides some religious overtones: "Housing lottery angst pervades campus... Students have been spotted with good-luck charms, have been known to either praise or curse various deities as the need arises,.... We're nervous because we don't know our chances. Obviously we don't want to be broken up, and we don't want to live on College Road," This is a simple statement of the reality of the lottery process, overlaid with 'angst' about who you might be sharing with. It is interesting to see quasi-religious elements creeping in.

From **Brown** (*ivygateblog.com*, Mar 2007) university comes the most over-blown comment I've seen so far:

> **Brown Housing lottery slightly less inhuman than most:** The housing lottery is one of the crueler systems ever devised, up there with the Spanish Inquisition and natural selection. Destroyers of friendships, sowers of schism, lotteries dehumanize you in ways that make the college admissions process look warm and fuzzy. Merit is meaningless; finagling, impossible. You become a number. You pray for better living and the lottery stares back with a cold, dull eye.

The only sensible conclusion from this set of haphazard extracts is that students treat the lottery as an enormous joke, something to be scoffed at. Conspicuously absent is a rejection of the lottery as such, as a means of allocating housing, or advocacy of alternatives.

One final piece from **Kenyon** College student newspaper merits attention because it picks up on cheating in the lottery:

> **Res Life aims to curb lottery cheating:** One rumored cheat is said to be that some students work with a student illegally living off campus. The student in need of the illegal student's better number or room would often offer to pay some of the overall housing cost in exchange for the preferred room. Another way to manipulate the old system was for two groups to switch roommates with one another to ensure good lottery numbers for both parties. Then, the original roommates would pair back up the day after the lottery.

Some things never change, but it shows how administrators need to be alert to possible malfeasance.

Insights from the 'natural experiment' of student housing lotteries

Insight 1: Consumers changing their preferences
A core tenet of the advocates of choice is that consumers know what they want and would like to be free to choose it. By satisfying these pre-ordained preferences all customers will thereby maximise their utility, leading to greater 'happiness' all round. But are consumers' preferences fixed, let alone knowable? If the answer is "no" then this blows a major hole in the economists' theory of demand.

Allocating student housing by lottery is a good example of thwarted consumer choice. This should lead to a significant loss of satisfaction compared to a situation where students could pick and choose. In a cleverly constructed study Dunn, Wilson & Gilbert (2003) yet again take advantage of the natural experiment unwittingly provided by use of the lottery. They canvassed the views of a large group of students (at which university is not stated, but it looks like Harvard) who went through a dictatorial random allocation of their student housing.

They were first asked, just before the allocation to rate how happy they might be if they 'won' a place at any of the 12 housing units. (The authors use 'happy' and 'happiness'; generally the less loaded description of 'Subjective Well-Being' is preferred by economists. There are obvious measurement difficulties, but social scientists are confident that they can reliably measure the 'happiness' of a subject at a given time, on a particular topic, as here with room-allocation.) How their happiness was affected by their actual allocation was monitored one and two years later.

The results were not what the economic theory would predict. Those who lost in the lottery and were forced to go into the *less desirable* accommodation were *happier*. It was vice-versa for those who won the better housing; they finished up less happy. The main reason for this discrepancy, the authors explain, is that students were focussing too much on the physical attributes of the property, ignoring the importance of the quality of their social life. This instability of customer tastes has been identified elsewhere, most notably by Khaneman (2003). The particular shift in consumer tastes described here could be described as "liking what you get" (as opposed to getting what you like). Customers who were forced to accept an alternative may find that they adapt to it and may finish preferring it to their original choice.

This sends a positive signal to administrators who might be tempted to try lottery allocation. The draw may produce winners who feel lucky to get into their preferred housing and losers who are disappointed. But with the passage of time things even up. Both winners and loser should adapt to their surroundings and it won't make much difference to their happiness. The usual caveat is that this 'natural experiment' was performed on an elite group of students. The results may not be transferrable, but other research elsewhere suggests that it would be.

Insight 2: Peer group effects:

Do students affect each others' behaviour? Does good behaviour rub off on those sharing the same space. 'Yes' is the answer according to this imaginative piece of research, yet another result which could only come from the 'natural experiment' of random allocation – in this case of student housing. Bruce Sacerdote (2000) of Dartmouth University examined the system established in 1994 (described above in Example (34b) above), where freshmen are assigned to dorms and roommates randomly. This was a manual system involving form-filling and paper-shuffling. The detail of the allocation procedure was important for Sacerdote to establish. He needed to show that this was a genuine randomised allocation procedure, just like they have in proper scientific trials. The curious feature of this lottery from the early 1990s is not only the initial lack of choice – students had to share with whomever the fickle finger of fate had decreed. Even more dictatorial was that post-allocation swaps were prohibited – which was good for the natural experiment if not for student satisfaction.

Apart from the historical value of this example, Sacerdote was able to draw an interesting conclusion about the *educational* benefits of weak students sharing with brighter ones. The widely held belief that students can affect each others' performance is borne out by the evidence in this case. As Sacerdote puts it:

> I find that peers have an impact on grade point average and on decisions to join social groups such as fraternities. Residential peer effects are markedly absent in other major life decisions such as choice of college major. Peer effects in GPA occur at the individual room level whereas peer effects in fraternity membership occur both at the room level and the entire dorm level. Overall, the data provide strong evidence for the existence of peer effects in student outcomes.

What he suggests is that should your under-achieving offspring be billeted with a high flyer, then offspring's grades should improve a little in the first year, without dragging down the high flyer. The effect though, is modest, and wears off by the final year. Nor should we overlook the fact that Dartmouth is an exclusive university; all students will be from higher brackets. Alas for researchers! The process currently used by Dartmouth in 2009, which is called the 'Room Draw' follows the standard pattern; the lottery merely determines your priority in the queue for choosing.

More general support for this peer-group effect comes from Beijing (example (19) which allocates school-places using a lottery. Fang Lai (2007) concludes that peers do affect performance; a policy of mixing students to avoid social stratification of school benefitted results overall. "Preliminary results find that decreased classroom diversity [as a result of lottery allocation] is beneficial to the student academic performance".

Insight 3: Thwarting strategic behaviour in room-allocation:
My third insight demonstrates what can go wrong and how theorists have suggested strategies for dealing with the situation. Delving back in time can produce some curious glimpses into some of the problems economists identify with non-market allocation systems, and the sometimes bizarre yet technically and mathematically clever solutions they proposed. Hylland & Zeckhauser (H&Z) (1979) both of Harvard were vexed by the behaviour of students in the housing allocation procedure at their university (already mentioned in Example (34b)). This was not initially a lottery-based system, but its introduction created an opportunity for disruptive behaviour:

> In 1976 and 1977 a rank-ordering procedure was employed. It was observed that a relatively small number of students were assigned to their first choice. ...The system was changed in 1977 that gave priority to first preferences, with individuals ordered by lot was introduced...Unfortunately this procedure generates strong incentives for strategic behaviour. For example, a student may list his second choice first if he thought his first choice would be listed first by many others. Hence he would give up a small chance of his first chance allocation for a high chance of his second choice. Harvard administrators did in fact believe that many students acted 'strategically' in 1977.

This may seem a trivial matter, and indeed it is in relation to student housing. (It may even be a useful lesson in life for the students involved – don't be gullible and believe everything you are told!) One obvious disadvantage from this strategic behaviour is that the suppliers of housing – the university authorities – get a false view of what students prefer. This may lead in turn to the production of new housing which is not the first preference of most students. Clearly this is an inefficiency that should be avoided.

Economists face this problem when designing procedures in other more important allocation issues, for example: when oil drilling leases are allocated (Haspel, 1990) or when radio frequencies are divided up between competing firms (Binmore & Klemper, 2002). Revealing, or causing the bidder to reveal their real preference is important in the process of ensuring the best allocation from a procedure, one which in the jargon is Pareto-optimal. In the case of Harvard and its student housing H&Z allude to the "prescribed distributional objectives" of the process. This may be to treat everybody equally, or to ensure that some individuals are systematically favoured. These objectives are not explained or justified, nor do they attempt to relate them to Harvard university policies or principles.

In their paper, with the aid of some impressive algebraic formulation they produce an improved lottery-based mechanism, which will still allow students to express their honest preferences for the housing on offer, but without encouraging strategic behaviour. Those with the requisite background in mathematical economics may wish to follow the full exposé of the idea by reading the original paper. To summarise H&Z's proposal: In essence what they propose is a pseudo-market. Individuals need to list not just their ordered preferences but how strongly they feel about each one. The mechanism then acts like a blind auctioneer, and 'purchases' a weighted lottery on behalf of each applicant. By sifting through these proposals it is possible to create an optimum weighted lottery which will maximise expected utility over all applicants. There is an impressive amount of illustration and game theoretic analysis to support this claim, but H&Z did not, it seems, take the final step – to try it out on an actual group of freshmen students.

As already seen the current (2009) Harvard room allocation system (34c) has little obvious opportunity for strategic behaviour. Nor, given the prohibition on post-allocation swapping does this achieves a Pareto-optimal distribution of student housing. Perhaps Harvard feels that a semi-random mixing of students fulfils educational objectives, as suggested by Sacerdote above, whatever evasion of consumer preferences might exist.

School systems, too, have had to deal with strategic behaviour, whether with the benefit of complex analysis or not is unclear, as this example shows:

'New lottery system foils crafty parents' (36) Boston Schools 2005
To prevent families from manipulating the system in trying to get their children into popular schools, the Boston School Committee approved a new computer lottery yesterday to assign students to schools. Under the new method, effective in 2006, the computer will cycle through all of a student's choices before moving onto the next student. Currently, the computer cycles first through the students' top choices. If a student does not live within the school's walk zone or have a sibling at the school, he stands little chance of getting in, if the school is popular. For a better shot at getting into a school they deem acceptable, parents list a less-popular school as their top choice – not their true first choice – in the annual student assignment lottery. Less-savvy parents who list only popular schools risk their children not getting into any school they choose. The computer then assigns them to schools with available seats. The school system hopes the new method encourages parents to be more honest about their choices. (*Boston Globe, Jul* 21, 2005)

Further evidence that 'gaming the system' can be found in school choice in the UK as well is given by Tough & Brooks (2007). In a survey it was found that nine per cent of parents in England did not express their genuine favourite school as their first preference. It was found that parents sometimes do not reveal their true preference in the belief that their preferred application would be unsuccessful and potentially leave them with a place in a school they had wished to avoid.

Chapter 11

Lotteries for Teachers: Sharing the Jobs

This chapter looks at the teachers, who are at the other end of the learning process from the students. I will produce a few examples of lotteries for teachers which mediate the way they are employed. This *could* have included hiring and promotion, and perhaps of most interestingly, work-sharing. But in this chapter I will mainly be describing 'lotteries which might happen'.

It all started because of a joke. While checking on some of the internet discussions about Brighton's school-place lottery I came across a blogger who had a bright idea. He suggested that putting large numbers of *parents* and pupils to trouble of shopping around and then travelling to their lottery-allocated school involved a lot of hassle. Would it not be better, he suggested, to swap the much smaller number of *teachers* around at random to different schools in the borough?

Yes, I'm sure it was meant to be a joke, but some of the best ideas start out as jokes. I had this experience when Martin Wainwright picked up on my proposals (Boyle, 1998) on using lotteries. His article, 'Lots of potential', appeared in *The Guardian* on April 1st, 1998. It was a serious description of the potential for lotteries to resolve tricky allocation disputes, and was most definitely not a spoof. The Guardian as with other newspapers try to include many such stories on April Fool's Day, some of which are decoys – stories which seem unbelievable, yet are actually true. Martin Wainwright is obviously intrigued by the topic, having written *The Guardian Book of April Fool's Day* (2007).

Sacking by lottery: Not a joke: This is the only example I have found of a lottery affecting teachers' jobs: **(37) Teacher sacking, Oregon 2009:** A report in *The Oregonian,* (May 10, 2009) explained how a lottery would decide layoffs. Using 'last in, first out' is often the basis for laying off staff when budget cuts strike. In Oregon because so many new teachers had started on the same day, there were dozens who shared the same length of service. By law Oregon State school districts are required to draw lots to break seniority ties. Individual districts then have to decide how to administer these lotteries. For example

> The Lake Oswego School District held its lottery [on May 8th], expecting to terminate 20 to 50 first- and second-year teachers.. The district's human resources director and the teachers union president gathered with a few witnesses, including two probationary teachers, to determine which teachers with equal seniority are likely to get pink slips. The director simultaneously drew a name and a number, then switched turns as the union president did the same.

It is re-assuring here to see a lottery which is conducted openly in way that precludes any accusation of fraud or fixing. As usual, the high state of emotion of potential victims was recorded; even the feelings of administrators was noted that:

> .. school officials acknowledge the human toll of turning people's livelihoods into a game of chance. "It's uncomfortable," said Winn, the human resources director. "We don't want to do this. It's emotional. Nobody wants to be the last person on the list." Earlier Ms Winn noted the strain of performing the actual draw: "My stomach hurts, but we did it."

Potential for lottery use in teacher employment: Oregon was a rare recorded example of teacher firing by lottery, but I would not be surprised to find it happening elsewhere. Human Resources managers in education might like to draw on experience of lottery use in other fields of public sector employment:

Hiring: Short-listing by lottery: Examples where a large field of applicants is reduced to a much smaller one include: Court Usher jobs in Northern Ireland, 2005 (in an advertisement *www.courtsni.gov.uk*) and for Police jobs in Gloucestershire (*Daily Mirror,* Sep 22, 2006).

The police example has its own sorry saga however. When an applicant was told that he had been "rejected by a lottery", he investigated further. In fact he had been rejected for being a white man. The police force in question wished to re-balance its ethnic and gender profile. The lottery was a cover story, and quite untrue. Ironically, the force in question *has* got provision for randomized short-listing in its procedures.

Some of these short-listing by lottery procedures have been tested in tribunals and have passed as acceptable. Generally though this process is used for low-level jobs, or so the available reports seem to indicate. It would be a big step to introduce short-listing by lottery for school-teaching positions. Sometimes educational vacancies attract a very large field of applicants. Reducing the field by means of a lottery could be a sensible option, so long as it is done honestly.

Firing: Sacking by lot: We have seen one example from Oregon of teacher sacking by lot. Other examples can be found in the literature, too. In China the old state-run industries needed to shed huge numbers as the economy prospered. (Estache & al, 2004 for details on this). In the UK sacking by lot has been tested in employment tribunals, and as with short-listing by lot has been found to be legal (p63-4, Boyle, 2006). The advantage of lottery layoffs for the organization is the avoidance of corruption (or the agency problem as the economists explain it). An incompetent employee might bribe the HR administrator to keep them on; this would not be in the interest of the organization. Lottery sacking may also help the organisation avoid costly and time-consuming tribunals and appeals.

The downside, as noted with the Oregon school-teachers' example is that ignores the merits of the individual teacher. The school may lose out by this, and an individual be unduly penalised. However, in China the intention was to release talent from old nationalised industries into the more productive parts of the economy. But if sacking is to be based on 'Merit' that begs the question: Can the performance of teachers be judged and ranked in a reliable manner?

Hypothetical (joke) lottery: Swap teachers around at random: I started this chapter with what was intended to be a joke. Instead of pupils being assigned by lottery to different schools, what if there was a lottery to decide which teachers went to each school? Let's take this idea seriously for a moment an examine its advantages:

For children and their parents: Children would be able to attend their nearest school, without losing contact with their friends from primary school. Proximity is seen by parents and others (Burgess et al, 2009) as the fairest means of deciding who is admitted to a particular school. With children going to their nearest school, there will be far less travelling around, less traffic on the roads. (As any commuter can attest, traffic flows are much worse during term-time mornings). This would benefit the environment.

For teachers: The 'best' teachers tend to cluster into the 'best' schools, because that is a matter of mutual preference between both school and teacher. (I leave out of account those dedicated teachers with a mission to help the less advantaged in Society.) If the skills of the 'best' teachers were to be deployed, at random, throughout the borough then the teachers would gain from the wider experiences, with a more diverse range of pupils. This could have the effect of shaking up and reviving their talents and enthusiasm for the job. It might also build 'team spirit' amongst the whole teaching staff, and underpin efforts to raise standards for all the children throughout the borough. Talented teachers would also have an opportunity to share their insights and wisdom more widely.

For the politicians: With teachers' talents spread evenly to all parts of the borough, all pupils would then have an equal chance of being taught by mumbling duffers as well as the Jean Brodies of the teaching profession. This could be seen as achieving a form of equality of opportunity. There is a downside when all attend their local school: There would be less social mixing, leading to less of the peer-group effects that seems to be so beneficial.

In the workplace: Sharing assignments out amongst the teaching staff: I know of no example where school-teachers are allocated at random to their classes, either within the school, or across the borough, although I have one small example from the field of training: **(38) Sharing out teaching assignments, training co-operative, London 2006:**   In London due to traffic congestion many adults are taking up cycling again for the first time since their childhood. To encourage them a day's training in road-craft is available. In one such adult cycle-training co-operative, where my son is a member, he tells me that new assignments are shared out by a daily lottery.

Beyond the realms of education and training, however, sharing jobs around within an organisation have been reported:

Coalminers' Cavil (Beynon & Austrin, 1994): In the Victorian times the coalmines in Durham and Northumberland in the North-East of England shared out pitches on a quarterly basis by means of the 'cavil'. This was a lottery system which decided who worked which part of the coalface for the next three months. The miners were paid per ton for what they extracted, so earning potential was significantly impacted by the ease of working. This varied throughout the mine, so the solution, with the co-operation of the miners' trade union was to share this out randomly.

In-shore fishermen's 'Padu' (Lobe & Berkes, 2004): In parts of Kerela fishing communities have established co-operatives. A major activity is the sharing out of stretches of the shore-line for fishing. This is done on a regular basis using a lottery called the 'Padu'.

Judges to court cases (Samaha, 2008):   In the US it is customary for judges to be allocated to their cases making use of a lottery. This practice is widespread and is used to avoid any suggestion that judges with a particular axe to grind are given one type of case, or that a defendant, because of the heinousness of their alleged crime, is given a particularly strict or lenient judge. It seems particularly appropriate that random allocation is used regularly as part of the processes of justice, given that the jury, the cornerstone of the Common Law is formed by the random selection of 12 citizens. According to Samaha these judge-allocating lotteries occur on a daily basis right across the US, and so may be the most widespread and frequent use of non-gambling lotteries in the world.

Instead of assigning teachers at random to their classes,
maybe students could be assigned randomly to teachers:
This is equally possible, and would have much the same effect. Here are a couple of examples, not from main-stream schools, but in a similar situation:

(39) Places on Courses for Elders, Chicago 2005: When there are more registrants who indicate a 'lotteried' seminar/workshop as their first choice than the spaces available, 5CLIR has devised a lottery system as the fairest method of allotting the available spaces to the participants. (*5CLIR Reporter,* Jan 2005)

(40) Choral training, Berkshire, US 2005: This is a not-for-profit educational institution which provides choral training:

> Experience has taught us that the lottery is the fairest method of determining the assignment of singers to the various BCF weeks [of choral training]. The lottery is a totally random selection of names, which gives every singer an equal chance of being accepted.... Please keep in mind a few vital statistics that we feel are important for you to know. The lottery procedure has been in practice for 10 years. During this time the percentage of people who were not drawn for any week in the lottery two years in a row is 1.23%. The percentage of people who were chosen for their 1st choice week is 94.5%. (from *chorus.org 2005*)

(41) Popular options, Stanford University 2009: When there are too many students seeking to take popular options on a university course, numbers may be controlled by means of a lottery. This procedure is reported by Stone (2009) at his own university of Stanford and he believes that many others universities follow the same procedure.

So lottery assignment of students to teachers happens, is not unusual and does not seem to be at all controversial. This is not the same as ensuring that each teacher is presented with a random class of students drawn from the student body. There is no opportunity therefore of drawing on a 'natural experiment' from these cases. This lack of validated knowledge makes the following question difficult to answer:

Do teachers matter anyway?

Of course we can all remember a truly inspirational teacher, as well as the teacher who turned you off his subject for the rest of your life! However obvious, the notion that some teachers can achieve higher grades from their students than others needs to be tested. In an informative and suggestive paper entitled 'Do teachers matter?' Slater, Davies & Burgess (2009) examine the evidence. As the title suggests, they ask if some teachers are better than others in getting higher grades for the pupils they teach. These researchers at Bristol draw on previous work carried out in the US where, controversially, some teachers are paid by results. In an attempt to screen out the effects of pupil variability the administrators of this scheme use VAM – value-added methodology – to identify which teachers are performing better.

It would be ideal for those researching into teacher performance if pupils *were* to be assigned randomly within the school to the teachers. This would provide the basis for a credible scientific experiment and eliminate the bias that might come from, say, good teachers being systematically allocated to the better classes. It would seem to be an interesting and perhaps even non-controversial procedure to allocate teachers at random to their classes, but I have found no record of it happening.

This does not deter researchers and others from attempting to do the calculations. They believe that they can control for the variations in student ability that might otherwise corrupt measures of teacher effectiveness. Rothstein (2009) disagrees "Because students are not even approximately randomly assigned to schools, these comparisons are likely to be less informative about causal effects than are the within-school comparisons considered here."

For those interested in following up the results from these researches and what they say about the variability in effectiveness between teachers (and the likelihood that the economists' fantasy that an incentive scheme based on payment-by-results could, on its own, raise student attainments) this briefly is what the papers referred to previously conclude:

Rothstein: Results for the US indicate that policies based on these VAMs will reward or punish teachers who do not deserve it and fail to reward or punish teachers who do. He also finds that conventional measures of individual teachers' value added fade out very quickly and are at best weakly related to long-run effects.

Slater & al: found for the UK that there was considerable variability in teacher effectiveness, a little higher than the estimates found in the few US studies. They also corroborate recent findings that observed teachers' characteristics explain very little of the differences in estimated effectiveness. They show that teachers matter a great deal: being taught by a high quality (75th percentile) rather than low quality (25th percentile) teacher adds 0.425 of a GCSE point per subject to a given student,

Beware the methodological flaws in these studies! They are not based on any form of randomised experiment. Slater et al may claim to have overcome these problems, although gaining 0.4 of a grade point extra (on average) is a worthwhile but hardly an enormous difference between a 'top' teacher's effect and a 'bottom' one. As Rothstein points out such effects soon fade. All authors are quick to remind readers that they are measuring just one variable, that of educational attainment as shown by test scores. Omitted and thus ignored are all the other contributions a teacher might make to a child's long-term educational experience, as well as the teacher's contribution to the wider school community. For a definitive scientific answer we must await random allocation of teachers to schools, and within schools to classes.

To finish this chapter which has dealt with some uncomfortable topics, let's look at a couple of more light-hearted themes which could make teachers' jobs a little easier.

A simple idea: using the lottery as a teaching aid: (42) Picking students at random to answer questions: *PICK ME! Sticks.* These are simple flat wooden sticks, one for each student. Teacher writes the name of each student on a stick, which are then all kept in a container. When the time comes for class participation, the teacher simply reaches for the *PICK ME! Sticks* container, chooses one at random and then calls the student's name found on the stick. Simple! (*prioritizerelationships.com/pickmesticks*)

And finally, a serious proposal by an eminent Victorian: Examination grades by lottery: In 1888 Edgeworth, the renowned Irish economist and statistician suggested that degree classification at Cambridge was already "something of a lottery". Degree classifications were not precisely determined and were subject to measurable variability. He went on to suggest that it would be easy to contrive a solemn conclave of the Fellows who would settle doubtful case by drawing lots. But, as he put it

> A public examination is already a sort of lottery of the graduated species, one which the chances are not equal, but are better for the more deserving... It is a species of sortition infinitely preferable to the ancient method of casting lots for honours and offices.

Edgeworth's use of 'graduated' is similar to the idea of a weighted lottery described elsewhere in this book. You may wish to find out for yourself about this 'ancient method of casting lots for offices' which was the basis of democracy for the classical Athenians. Oliver Dowlen's (2008) *The political potential of sortition* gives a very good description of this. But grades of degree by lottery is surely a step too far?

Edgeworth returned in 1890 to his theme, concerned about entry examinations for the Civil Service.

> Serious differences of income and position could turn upon differences of marks which are largely or altogether accidental. This

would impose hardship on those just outside the gates of Paradise...The general recognition of the element of chance in examinations would mitigate the disappointment.

Edgeworth then suggests that what is needed is not a random shake-up of the marks, but a graduated entry lottery. Candidates would be given tickets proportional to their examination scores. Neither the State nor the Civil Service would lose out, claimed Edgeworth, because, *ex hypothesi*, in the long run the same proportion of really deserving candidates would be appointed. The benefits of such a process would be two-fold: the sense of injustice felt by the candidates would be mitigated; and the public would be alerted to the aleatory (dice-like) character of the examinations.

Needless to say Edgeworth's proposals were not taken up at the time, but his idea of a graduated lottery for entry did turn up again in the selection of entrants for medical schools in the Netherlands.

Part IV:

Conclusions: Lotteries for Education

Chapter 12

Lottery Practicalities: How it Should be Done

Practical lotteries: So you want to use a lottery to decide who to reject and who to award with that coveted school or university place? In this chapter I would like to make a few practical points about running a lottery. The aim should be to achieve the result that the administrators want, while at the same time satisfying the wishes of the various clients involved. Since most of this takes place in the public sector then simple 'customer satisfaction' surveys are not enough. When using the lottery the collective, public values of justice and fairness are also involved. Administrators ought to strive to achieve this, but they must always be aware of the downside: what would happen if things go wrong, if there is a complaint? In these litigious times bureaucrats have to be on their guard against possible legal suits of malpractice.

Point 1. Producing the random numbers: Reliable, checkable and cheat-proof mechanisms: As seen in the many examples, the random numbers can be produced by old-fashioned mechanical means but the modern method is to "use a computer". Both methods have their pitfalls:

Mechanical randomisation devices include the age-old gambler's tools of dice, decks of cards, roulette wheels or the favourite one is by the drawing of balls from an urn or cage. These can be ping-pong balls (with numbers marked on) which may be blown up in the air and caught. It may be a set of numbered balls in a bag, with a trusted person (often a child) pulling balls from a bag. The deluxe version of The Balls is used by the National Lottery in the UK.

Electronic devices started life with machines like ERNIE – the Electronic Random Number Indicating Equipment – which depended on the spin of electrons. This is a rare example of one of nature's truly random events. It is still in use today:

> Since 1957, the four generations of ERNIE have produced the numbers for over 110 million tax-free prizes worth over £7 billion. The basic function of each ERNIE machine has not changed but, with continuous advances in technology, each ERNIE has been replaced by a faster and smaller model to keep pace with Premium Bond demand. (*www.nsandi.com/products/pb/surprisingfacts*)

These days most administrators rely on PRANGs – Pseudo-Random Number Generators. These are computer programs (algorithms) which can be made to produce a stream of random numbers. For example, if you are using a spreadsheet you can insert a command to produce random numbers in whatever range, distribution and quantity needed.

Maybe the 'Pseudo' part of PRANG should make you concerned that these are not genuine random numbers, and would not be safe to use to decide who gets the school or university place. Fear not! Although any random-number generating computer program can produce the same stream of numbers if it is 'seeded' with the same initial number, usually there is some in-built mechanism to make the output look truly random (like taking the last two digits from the clock as seed). You can also rely on the fact that the PRANGs provided with standard packages have been thoroughly tested. There is a whole sub-genre of mathematics which looks at patterns in the numbers produced to prove if they are truly like a set of randomly produced numbers.

Mechanical devices like those used in the National Lottery can also be tested. Much effort has been put into discovering the 'hot numbers' – numbers which seem to turn up more often. This is based on the theory that the sets of balls that are used have slight imperfections, and these might cause some numbers to come up more often than others. Of course there will always be slight variations in ball size and weight, but they should not be so great as to affect the outcome in an observable way. It is the job of the National Lottery promoters to ensure that no consistent pattern of 'hot' or 'cold' numbers will turn up; their machinery should have been well tested before being used. One hears less from these 'numbers analysts' these days, mostly because they have discovered that in the long run there are no 'hot' numbers. The machinery for major draws like the UK National Lottery can be accepted as reliably random.

But there have been cases where bias, the statisticians term for deviation from randomness, has been alleged and proven. A notorious example was the 1970 US military draft. This was based on birth-dates, so that 366 balls containing a unique day of the year were placed in the 'gold fish bowl'. But something went wrong. Those with birthdates later in the year were picked more than pure chance would indicate. On investigation it was found that the balls had been put in a box in month order, with January first. The subsequent mixing efforts were insufficient to overcome this sequencing. (Based on a description of this controversy which has been turned into an exercise for students of statistics at website of the American Statistical Association. Also Fienberg 1973)

Another possibility is that an outright blunder has been made and not noticed: I have heard of an Australian case where newly built social housing was distributed to applicants by drawing a numbered card from a deck (The Star-Bowcott housing initiative). The cards were kept in a box which was dropped and the cards fell out. Accidentally a few of the cards were missed and not returned to the box. It was many draws later before this shortfall was discovered!

But what if there is an attempt at outright cheating? There are many reports (Finlay, 1980; Queller, 1977) of dastardly dealings from the lottery carried out in the old city-state of Venice over many years. This was the original 'ballota' — the drawing of balls from an urn to decide which member of the elite would land which plum job. Cheating took several forms, the favourite one of which seemed to be the 'ball up the sleeve' stunt, as a way of introducing a favourable ball for you or your client.

Children seemed to have had a pivotal role in ensuring that no chicanery went on, on the grounds, I suppose, that their youth and innocence made them immune from being suborned. They were used in Venice, as well as for the original British National Lottery (which was suppressed in 1823 after many years dubious service). Hicks (2009) tells of the boys from the London Bluecoat school who were pressed into service, and were not entirely immune from fraud.

Cheating, bias in the machinery or program or even accidental tinkering with the mechanism can all upset the process of randomisation. Of course the administrators must take all necessary precautions to avoid these deformations. They must get it right, and must be seen to get it right. This is one reason why the draw should be done in public, in plain view. It is why an 'innocent' should make the crucial selection. These build confidence. It is vital too, that the numbers produced are published, so that statisticians can check to see if there has been any deviation from apparent true randomness. Of course all this confidence is much more difficult to achieve if the numbers are produced "by a computer".

I am constantly un-nerved by casual comments in the descriptions of lottery-choosing that "the random numbers are chosen by a computer", or "the draw is carried out in an office by a notary" (as Professor Drenth informed me of earlier version of the Dutch medical school entry draw). I have no doubt that the people carrying out these draws are honest and scrupulous in ensuring that it is a fair draw, that no-one has interfered with it, that the randomisation mechanism or algorithm is valid, and has been tested to be fair, so that the winners and losers can rely on the results. The core difficulty is inherent in the lottery process: it is meant to be a sudden, non-reversible cut-off event. Once the random numbers have been produced, or the balls drawn, there is no trace of how it was done. This is 'blind chance' and leaves no audit trail. If a disgruntled victim of a lottery-choice feels that some chicanery went on then there is no way that they can be re-assured, especially if the draw is done in private or the numbers have been produced by some mysterious computer. Unless the draw was done openly, with some form of independent testing possible then there can always be doubt. It is for this reason that many schools use trustworthy outside agencies like the Electoral Reform Society to carry out the actual draw.

Point 2. Who is included in the draw? Entry restrictions, real and practical: There can never be a pure lottery, that is to say one where the only decision to select or reject is made by the luck of a draw. There will always be some form of entry restriction for any educational lottery whether for schools or colleges. In the case of universities this may well be an academic hurdle, such as obtaining a certain number of grades, maybe in specified subjects. But what about home-based or overseas students? It is not usual to admit both groups through the same process. For schools which are designated 'comprehensive', and which aim to cater for the community as a whole the restrictions are less clear-cut. Apart from the obvious limitation of needing to prove the age of the child, there may be catchment area restrictions. Faith-based schools may apply a religious test. Even where schools have an academic criterion for entry, this may be a threshold, which once surpassed entitles the applicant to a chance of entry.

All of these actual limitations on entry should be easily understood by applicants, hence the requirement that schools and colleges set them out clearly and communicate them. This is where the hypothetical freedom to apply for admission and hard reality clash. Posting these entry requirements on the school website is good; posting the entry rules in an envelope to potential applicants would seem to be quite enough to give everyone a chance.

But there still remains the misgiving that on the one hand schools will make the rules more opaque than necessary, and on the other that some parents are too dim or insufficiently motivated to try to understand the rules. It is for this reason that the discussions on the English Code for school admissions suggested that 'choice advisors' should be employed at each school to help parents, especially those from disadvantaged backgrounds. Their job would be to help parents navigate their way through the choice-with-lottery system. One particular anxiety was that some parents would be intimidated by the bureaucracy and lack the confidence to apply for better schools. Choice advisors, it was hoped, would stiffen their resolve.

Point 3. A Simple single lottery, or banding and several lotteries?
One response to the dilemmas posed by the perceived lack of pushiness by some parents is to rig the lottery in their favour. However theoretically fair to all applicants any system of lottery selection might be, there are still those who feel it is not enough. Tough & Brooks (2007) feel that banding must also be applied: that the applicant cohort should be divided up by some test of ability, such as performance on a KeyStage test or by the socio-economic status of the parents. A similar problem, though a less acute one can be found in weighting schemes like the one use for Dutch medical school entry.

How are the bands to be devised? Should the bands be divided up according to the school's current intake, or by its traditional catchment area, or by the whole of the local education authority area, or even the country as a whole? These are not trivial distinctions. For the Dutch university scheme a simple mathematical formula converted numerical scores into letter grades A, B, C, D, E, F. No attempt was made to produce equal numbers in each grade.

On the basis of the bands for school entry, a quota will be drawn from each to fill up the places. Choosing from within each band can then proceed using a lottery. This seems to have been done at Lady Margaret School (5), which resulted in 12 separate lotteries. As the Schools Adjudicator pointed out, this makes it difficult for an individual parent to figure out their chance of success in this multiplicity of lotteries.

Whatever banding scheme is chosen there will always be incentives to 'game the system'. Lady Margaret School tried to avoid this by telling parents that the details of the lottery are unimportant, and all that matters is that it is a game of chance. If, as the Adjudicator proposes, the school comes clean about its banding, and makes the details of its multiple draws public, then, as I suggested before, possibilities to game the system emerge.

Point 4. Dealing with bad luck: Whilst the administrators of lottery-selection schemes must be aware that the applicants might get up to crafty strategic behaviour to gain an unfair advantage, other applicants may cry foul because the lottery has been especially unkind to them. This could be called the 'Meike Vernooij' syndrome, when a very high scoring student, very keen to study medicine, that Erasmus University was keen to accept, still failed to get on to the course. It was her very bad luck to be rejected *three* times by the medical school entry lottery. She really was unlucky, if we use the figures quoted by Drenth. With an 80% chance of success at each entry stage, she was more than 99% certain of getting in on three attempts.

Such was the furore at this unlikely turn of events, and such was the successful publicity campaign mounted on her behalf that the Drenth Commission was set up to examine her predicament. Such minute chances of losing may suggest that "hard cases make bad law". But just as with the National Lottery, when there is a big enough pool of competitors then even the remotest of chances will strike *somebody* sooner or later. Although Drenth found that the existing system was sound on the basis of the facts he uncovered, he accepted the need to avoid such extreme bad luck.

The politicians agreed. After 1998 students like Meike Vernooij were to be 100% certain of a place. A consequence which was less-well appreciated was that many more adequately-qualified students who may have been just as highly motivated had their chances of medical school entry diminished. In fact, according to Goudappel (1999), the Dutch system has always kept back a small number of places to deal with 'hard luck' cases like

Meike Vernooij. She had appealed, but the authorities had not been convinced of her merits (using the standard old-fashioned interview and reporting techniques, one assumes).

Bureaucratic discretion is, perhaps, the best way of dealing with such extreme bad luck. It is inevitable in any lottery selection system that such rare events will happen. It might be possible to invent a lottery cascade which gives losers in one round a better chance next time. This could operate in the borough-wide centralised admissions schemes, but would be a bureaucratic nightmare when each school or separate authorities acted independently. It may be messy to retain an element of bureaucratic discretion in the system; it flies in the face of all the carefully crafted reasons for adopting the neutral, fair and incorruptible method of lottery. But any human system will throw up unforeseen anomalies, so a small amount of discretion seems like a sensible and practical fix.

Point 5. Should siblings and other special cases get priority?
There remains one anomaly in nearly all school-entry systems. If, as a parent you already have one child at the school, and another is of an age to apply, child number two has automatic entry. There is clear unfairness in this arrangement. Parents who are already privileged with one child at a good school are then doubly blessed with another place. (It can be safely assumed if they do not like the school for the first child they would be free to choose any other school.)

Allowing privileged access for siblings creates an opportunity for cheats as well as the following example shows: **(43) Sibling scam at Chicago magnet lottery school 2008:** At Sabin Magnet School, Chicago a scam involved making false claims that children had siblings at the school. This was an effort to get preference for admission. The school operated a lottery entrance procedure, but with the usual automatic entry for siblings. An instructor assistant had altered the application of at least one child to claim that he was a brother of the clerk's niece, although they were not related. The assistant had also encouraged another parent to claim on an application that his or her child was a sibling of a student already enrolled at the school. (*Chicago Tribune, Feb* 3, 2008)

I do not suggest overturning the sibling rule although clearly discriminates against smaller families or those with widely spaced births. There is obviously strong political support for it. I merely wish to draw attention to a curious anomaly.

Point 6. Remember customer satisfaction with the process: We have already seen the instant reactions of people when asked about the idea of random allocation of places at schools and universities. They don't like it. This was the reaction to Carnevale & Roses's (2003) survey. Even the survey about school places by lottery (Sutton Trust, 2007) showed little enthusiasm for the idea at first. This would seem to suggest that a lottery is a bad idea, not the process that would satisfy the customers. But the Sutton Trust went a bit further. When the question was 'framed' and when the less attractive alternatives were proposed then the respondents grew to appreciate the virtues of lottery choosing.

Economists are generally indifferent as to *how* customers get hold of the products they receive; all that matters is the *value* of the product. But in some practical research by Anand (2001) he found that people do indeed place different values on alternative ways in which scarce goods could be shared out. Procedural fairness has a value, which gives an additional reason for adopting lottery selection. People place a value on the fairness of the *procedures* which are used to distribute benefits, as well as whatever they derive from the procedure.

Anand canvassed the opinions of a random group of British voters, in particular on the use of lottery allocation of scare goods. He tested views on the *fairness* of the use a lottery to resolve a difficult medical decision. Here is the question he put to his panel of voters:

> **Scenario:** Two adults arrive at casualty with a life-threatening condition that does not affect their ability to make decisions. The doctor explains that there are resources only to treat one patient and then proposes that she will decide which one is to be treated by *tossing a coin.*

*Q1: If you were one of the patients, would you think that a **doctor's choice** based on a coin toss was a fair way of choosing which patient to treat?:*

*Q2: Alternatively: same question but this time the **patients toss** the coin?:*

The responses to these two questions show a different reaction to what are essentially the same the same circumstances and an identical prize. Neither process was thought to be 'fair'. From this and other evidence Anand makes a much more general claim that "there is strong lay resistance to random choosing as a fair process". His explanation for this is that random choosing deprives customers and clients of some control or 'voice' in the process. There is a further twist to the survey. If his survey respondents did not like choices being made by the doctor by the toss of a coin, they reacted even more negatively to the idea of the patients doing the tossing. Allowing the patients do the coin-tossing only added to the perceived unfairness of the process.

So whether a lottery or some other means of distribution is used can contribute to the perceived value of the process. But even if a lottery is to be used, the form it takes can also matter. In Anand's example transferring the burden of making the toss to the victim was resented. Better to have the perpetrator, in this case the doctor, take responsibility for the fateful toss. These details matter.

Point 7. Should the draw be public or private? Social cohesion: Ceremony has been used by humans for millennia to mark important events like births and weddings. Bringing people together seems to fulfil an important role in 'social cohesion' to use the current buzz-word. From some of the reports of public draws, for example Baltimore (7) or even students being allocated their housing in a lottery (34) they have the effect of gathering those affected by the draw together for a shared event. Even Edgeworth's (1890) advocacy of examination grades by lottery suggested a "solemn conclave of the fellows" where the actual drawing would take place. For the centuries-long tradition of choosing two leaders by lot, the republic of San Marino held the annual draw in the main basilica during Sunday Mass, with a child from the congregation pulling out the names. (Aubert, 1959)

When the draw is in public it is possible to *see* all of the applicants' names being put into the bowl/urn/cage prior to the drawing out of the names. It was disappointing to discover that Lancashire (1) carried out the draw in secret. Being there, seeing the result of a lottery would be much more fun, as well as a lot easier to understand (pun intended!). There could be no more efficacious means of promoting social cohesion than by holding the draw in public.

To summarise the points

1. Hold the draw openly, or use a trusted organisation to do it. Publish the numbers and encourage scrutiny.
2. There should be clear rules governing eligibility to enter the draw, with information easily available (plus choice advisors?)
3. Consider whether to use a single lottery, or introduce banding and many lotteries.
4. Anticipate the treatment of the very unlucky applicants.
5. Should special categories like siblings continue to get priority.
6. Remember that satisfaction with the process has a value.
7. Consider the benefits of a draw held in public as a ceremony.

The witty front cover of the 1997

'Drenth' Report on weighted lotteries

Chapter 13

To Conclude: Lotteries for Education: Yes or No?

Using lotteries to decide who wins a place at a good school or on a desirable college course remains contentious, more so in the UK than in the US. Having trawled through a wide range of examples of lotteries in use and looked at some of the scientific inferences that others have drawn from and about them, it is high time to draw some conclusions of my own. It is time to address the question: can a lottery be the right mechanism to decide who wins the educational prize?

At first glance the answer would seem to be clear-cut. For comprehensive education which caters for the whole population then a lottery is an acceptably democratic mechanism. For educational places which are academically selective, and this must include places at universities, then a lottery seems nonsensical. Not all schooling is comprehensive; in England there remains a residual grammar-school system which selects academically at age 11. Nor is all higher education systematically selective on academic ability: Opportunity and access to higher education has spread to nearly half of 18 year olds in the UK, more even in the US. Many courses will then admit a more 'comprehensive' intake, while insisting on adequate minimum standards. Good examples of this were the para-medical courses of nursing at Glendale, California (29) and physiotherapy at Leeds and Huddersfield (30).

So my conclusion seems to be that lotteries would be generally appropriate in sharing out school and college places in a comprehensive system, but would be wrong when entry by academic selection is required and the need is to pick potential winners for higher achievement. Somewhat perversely I am going to argue the opposite!

Time to abolish choice and the lotteries they spawn? I started in Part I by pointing out that the use of lotteries for school-places was almost entirely a consequence of the Choice Agenda: if there was to be no parental choice then there would hardly be any opportunity for the use of lotteries. There can be other ways of deciding who should get the places under the Choice Agenda, but lotteries have emerged as serious contenders for the 'best' (or maybe 'least-worst') method of resolving contentious over-subscriptions.

As we have seen, where choice plus a lottery has been established, this sometimes presents an interesting opportunity for analysis. Although not intended as such, the use of lottery selection can create a natural scientific experiment. Researchers, mainly in the US have been able to draw on this to test the effectiveness of parental choice in raising school standards. The results generally fail to substantiate the claim that choice raises educational attainment. Persuasive voices suggest that there is a consensus that choice does *not* work in achieving the objectives claimed for it. The Public Policy case for abolishing Choice seems to be well-founded, thanks to the fortuitous result of using lotteries to allocate school-places.

Nevertheless there are two important and influential groups who will cling to the 'commonsense' view that choice works:

Parents, who are sensibly concerned for the company that their child might keep at school. They will seek out the highest-scoring school in the league tables, even though they may be well aware that getting in to this school will do little for their child's grades. Middle-class parents prefer their children to attend schools with children similar to their own, or more specifically which are not 'over-run' by the lower orders. Such sentiments are not voiced but they exist nonetheless. And parents are not entirely wrong as

Sacerdote (34b) discovered: Brighter peers can upwardly influence the scores of the duller ones.

So school choice and what seems to be the inevitable lotteries will continue. Many parents may like the sense of empowerment ('voice' as Anand put it) that the exercise of choice seems to confer. Some parents might be against the idea of 'choice' because they find it a burden. Acquiring information, trekking around to check out potential schools, not to mention the long daily journeys to the school of choice if successful in gaining entry all have a cost. But choice, especially the opportunity to exercise it remains a persuasive idea with influential voters.

Politicians are attracted to 'choice' because, as Le Grand showed it is popular with the voters. Choice also seems to provide an easy mechanism to by-pass the messy, clunky business of making real improvements in education. It is also a handy stick to beat teachers and educational administrators by setting school against school. And there will always be the siren voices of out-dated free-market economists who will chant "choice works" despite the evidence to the contrary.

So choice for school places is likely to be with us for some time. It will continue to pose its inevitable consequence: that demand for places at a good school will always outstrip supply. Some mechanism other than proximity has to be found to share the perceived benefits provided by the public purse for the good of everyone. By that calculus a lottery becomes the 'necessary palliative'.

Lotteries for comprehensive places, or is there something better?

The features which make a lottery an attractive way to decide school places should be familiar by now. It is efficient, both for the schools and the children. It is manifestly fair, giving real equality of opportunity as far as possible throughout the borough.

But perhaps the main virtue of lottery selection is that it removes *all* forms of rationality both good and bad from the allocation process. This is what Stone (2007) calls its *sanitizing* effect. Dowlen (2008) uses the expression *arational* with much the same significance. On its own this does not seem like a sound reason for using lotteries, but in the face of many bad reasons for selecting entrants then a lottery shines through.

Amongst the *bad reasons* which the English School Code was designed to avoid would include: selection based on socio-economic status; selection which creams off the best students, depriving other schools of their uplifting talents; but worst of all (in the eyes of UK parliamentarians) was that entry had become dependent on the ability of parents to buy over-priced property in the catchment area. Blocking these bad reasons is certainly one consequence of lottery selection for school places.

But lotteries, when compared to most other forms of selection can have downsides:

– Schools usually have some speciality such as music, science or sport. Lotteries make it difficult to match pupils with schools.

– There might be a 'moral hazard' if the school-entry system becomes over-reliant on lotteries, and administrators cease to look for better, rational means of selection.

– For the victims of lottery selection the decision can be very abrupt. People, according to Elster (1989) value having *reasons* for decisions. It might even be more acceptable to have a faked or phoney reason for a decision rather than the overtly non-reasoned lottery.

– Lotteries scatter children around the borough, literally at random; this may break up some of the bonds that may exist a neighbourhood. Friendships and acquaintances are thereby broken; local communities lose a shared experience.

– With the constant drizzle of bad stories about 'post-code lotteries' then its use in school place allocation will seem to have sinister associations. Unfamiliarity, too, breeds suspicion.

– The unfairness and seeming illogicality of denying a school-place to a child who lives within short walking distance of the school is a theme which crops up repeatedly. Lotteries deny the traditional criterion of proximity.

Perhaps it is this last feature which may eventually scupper lotteries for school places. School choice requires parents to shop around for the best schools, not necessarily the nearest. The upshot is that swarms of children spend ages of time travelling on buses or in family cars, often driving past each other to distant schools. All this bus- or car-based travel is adding to global warming, and may soon be seen as anti-social as holidaying by air.

The use of lotteries for school places to wither away? From experience, once the initial excitement has died down then the need for lotteries seems to fall away. This was what has happened in Burnley in Lancashire (1). Perhaps parents have learnt that seeking out the 'best' schools does not greatly influence academic achievement. Children may often prefer to go to the local school, keeping in touch with their mates, ignoring the hypothetical but long-term advantages of better schools.

So perhaps the *use* of school place lotteries will become less prevalent, even if they remain a legitimate tactic for administrators to have in reserve. Holding the threat of a lottery over the heads of pushy parents may be enough to deter them; better the certainty of a school-place nearby than the uncertain outcome of random choosing.

Instead of a lottery: banding plus proximity? A system which directly achieves the social mixing that the politicians crave while reducing the cost and eco-burden of travelling has been mentioned already: this was banding-plus-proximity as proposed by Tough & Brooks (2007). Applicants are classified by some form of academic criteria into ability bands and a quota is declared for each band. Within each band those living nearest the school are accepted first. Already we have one example, the Haberdashers' Aske's school (4) which has dropped the lottery in favour of banding plus proximity.

Another, Lady Margaret (5) was using banding but with lottery selection within the bands. How the bands are established, and what are to be the quotas within bands could make a major difference to social inclusiveness and fairness, but overall I believe this, rather than lotteries, could the way forward for school choice .

Lotteries for academically selective courses; surely wrong?

General courses, with vocational bias: With the expansion of access to higher education there are many courses at universities and colleges which cater for a wide range of student abilities. Many of the courses are intended to produce well-trained and educated professionals in a range of skills. In a sense they are much like the 'comprehensive' schools described earlier. But admission is not open to all. Applicants still need to show they have *sufficient* ability to benefit from the course before being admitted. Admissions tutors may be tempted to limit entry using higher academic hurdles. This may be a convenient form of gate-keeping, but is another example of a *bad* reason, the sort which lotteries would block. For this reason the use of a lottery to select the student intake makes more sense: it enables opportunity to be spread more widely, and encourages students to exercise choice more widely too.

In this respect the example of nursing courses at Glendale (29) and physiotherapy course at Leeds and Huddersfield (30) show great wisdom. Rather than engage in useless and inappropriate interviewing, they fixed on an adequate entry level grade. In the case of Glendale this was backed up with research, which showed that higher grades were not required for students on that particular course. Using the false-merit technique of higher entry grades would also introduce other forms of discrimination. A simple lottery over all applicants who make this grade then seems to be an entirely fair method of choosing who to admit onto the course.

But is this inefficient? Critics might argue that accepting minimally-but-adequately qualified entrants will lead to greater drop-out rates. Because of the lottery too many students will undertake courses which are beyond them and too many expensive places funded by the taxpayer will be taken up by those who will fail. If the supply of manpower is to be maximised for the benefit of the economy as a whole, then lottery selection seems to be wasteful.

This may be so, but it needs to be demonstrated. Like so many 'obvious' conclusions by experts, things are not always what they seem. Before condemning lottery selection the evidence against it should be produced. Perhaps it might be the case that individual courses would achieve a higher pass rate by setting the entry barrier higher. This local efficiency would probably have the unintended consequence of discriminating against various groups.

It might also be the case that global efficiency would be better served by spreading the talent around (assuming that 'talent' for a particular profession can be identified by school-leaving grades). Achieving a profession which includes members of all groups in society is also a laudable aim. For this too, a lottery for all minimally-but-adequately qualified applicants would be effective, and probably far less costly and disruptive than alternative affirmative-action procedures.

Lotteries can sometimes produce freak results, so it may have been sensible that Huddersfield (30) adopted a quota lottery technique, in effect running three different lotteries for male, female and mature applicants. Generally though such a strategy is unwise. It introduces further and un-necessary complexity and spoils the simplicity of one-lottery-for-all. By privileging some groups it introduces a new form of discrimination.

But what if, say, the applicant group for nursing courses is overwhelmingly female, or applicants for plumbing or bricklaying courses are similarly overwhelmingly male? Innate differences exist and are recognised between genders (Baron-Cohen, 2003). This is not all a case of social conditioning. Professions may seek to achieve a better balance, not wishing to be closed off to certain groups, but different preferences will persist. If the results of a lottery selection process produces unbalanced entry classes, then it can reasonably be claimed that this is because of student preferences not discrimination (because the lottery has 'sanitized' out such bad reasons). Another positive feature of lottery-selection is that it would also encourage students to pursue non-traditional courses; like girls into building, boys into nursing. Since the entry is by lottery and is transparently open and unbiased no-one should feel intimidated when making an unusual (unusual for their gender anyway) application.

Elite courses*:* It might seem to be much more difficult to justify the use of lotteries for courses and at universities which traditionally and of necessity require highly pre-qualified applicants. These include the usual professional medical and legal courses, providing highly prestigious qualifications which lead to well-paid employment. For courses like dentistry and engineering numbers must be limited because of laboratory and workshop space. The best universities in the land are also intended to promote scholarship at the highest level. In such cases it would be ludicrous to suggest that they should draw from a pool of minimally qualified candidates to form their entry group. Academic selection, choosing the best and brightest must not be compromised for this elite set of courses.

If the college or university intends to achieve the highest rate of success with their intake then choosing those with the top entry grades is the simplest and most obvious strategy. As Drenth (see Chapter 8) and others have shown the higher the entry qualifications the better the final degree and the quicker it is achieved. The relationship is not perfect, but the trend is clear-cut. For elite courses with high academic ambitions the strategy seems to be to pick the top scorers at entry. So what if anything could justify lotteries for selective (elite) university places? I will take this difficult case in stages, starting with the most easily justified form of lottery-selection.

Borderline selection: We have already seen where universities use lotteries for borderline grades, as for example at some Irish universities (27). There will always be a minimum entry score and only rarely can all applicants at that minimum be accepted. Rather than engage in elaborate (and pointless) extra screening, or even worse, demanding more finely graded examination results, the use of a lottery is practical and efficient.

Inter-temporal fairness: Drenth provoked the Dutch educational authorities into reminding him of inter-temporal fairness. Drenth had suggested awarding automatic entry to the top 50% of applicants. The response was that it would be unfair to admit a C-grade one year and reject the same grade the following year, just because more As and Bs had applied. Instead, a fixed grade boundary was established: if you get in with a C grade this year, then in fairness all C grades should be given the same treatment from one year (or decade) to the next.

Applying such inter-temporal equality may often lead to there being more qualified applicants than places. If it was deemed that an A-level result of BBC was sufficient for admission one year it would be dishonest to claim that the same grade caused rejection in the following year. If there is excess demand from qualified applicants, then elite universities should, in fairness, deal with this by a lottery. Raising the entry barrier may improve the pass rate in the final examinations but is a dishonest and unfair method of dealing with excess demand.

Balance of risks: Use a weighted lottery: But should this go further? I have already expressed a preference for the Dutch weighted-lottery entry model that lasted from 1975 until 1998. But should it have gone further as I suggested in Chapter 9? It may sound somewhat idealistic to require universities to balance the risks with their applicant cohort, but given that access to elite courses confers huge advantages on the winners, then an egalitarian government should insist on it. The upshot would be a weighted lottery along the

Dutch medical school entry lines, but with weightings which gave even more encouragement to lower scoring applicants.

This may seem an outrageous dilution of educational standards, but remember that all applicants in the Dutch example at any rate are drawn from the top 10% of school leavers. All have a very high chance of succeeding; it is just that some have slightly more chance than others. Extending this group slightly would reach down to the 50/50 applicant – the one who on the basis of their entry grades has a 50% chance of succeeding on the course

Of course this marginal 50/50 applicant would have only a very scant chance of gaining entry, but at least he or she would not be given *zero* chance. Very high scoring candidates would be given correspondingly high chances, but could not automatically assume entitlement to a place. This strikes me as a wholly desirable corrective to the 'winner takes all' mentality.

Some local efficiency might be lost by using weighted lotteries, with slightly fewer professionals being produced. Efficiency needs to be weighed against Fairness. Since the 'prize' of a medical qualification leads to such great rewards both financially and in status, then the chance to achieve that should be shared fairly amongst qualified applicants from all parts of society. Only a weighted lottery can do this. A weighted lottery would be a manifestation of a fundamental democratic urge to fairly share the rewards.

Making sharing more practicable

Sub-divide the 'non-divisible' prizes: The case in fairness for the use of lottery-sharing has been repeatedly trumped by efficiency arguments. This arises because the goods on offer, such as places at an educational establishment are non-divisible. You are either accepted onto a medical course or you are not; you gain a place at a magnet academy school or you do not. That is the way the system works.

But with a bit of imagination it may be possible to sub-divide these prizes a bit more. Modularisation of university courses was supposed to lead to much more flexibility. This could apply equally to prestigious medical courses, where the current all-or-nothing courses could be further broken down into free-standing stages, with a worthwhile qualification at each stage. Schools, too, could cater for narrower age groups with transfer the next stage mediated by lottery.

If places at these courses and schools, now deemed to be 'non-divisible goods' were sub-divided as far as practicable then the efficiency arguments would lose much of their potency. Enrolment through the widest possible weighted lottery would have less of a downside, and opportunity spread more widely. More of those with specific talents for a profession, or a great enthusiasm for it would come through, not just the high entry-test scorers. It may also benefit late-developers and those who are unsure what they really want to do, or have an aptitude for.

Justice through life-time lotteries: Throughout this book all the analysis has been based on one-off lotteries. It is assumed that this novel approach might be used once in a person's lifetime, to select for a secondary school or a university place. This one-off procedure, as philosophers would be quick to point out, is not equality of opportunity. Some win, some lose. The only equality is that of the chance of winning.

But what if in a future 'Aleatoria' (to use Goodwin's (2005) delightful description) the logic of using lotteries is accepted and used for all the important decisions which affect one's life? In Aleatoria it is used to decide who gets into schools at all levels, who is admitted on to popular university courses. It extends to non-educational selection and allocation, which includes housing (just like the US student housing examples (34)). In Aleatoria lotteries would also used for jobs, to hire, fire and promote (with appropriate safeguards so that candidates lacking merit are excluded); again we glimpsed something of that in lotteries for teachers in Chapter 11.

In such an imaginary world your whole-life chances would be the sum of the outcomes of all the lotteries you have been through. Statisticians explain that a single toss of a coin comes out as either a head or tail, but if you keep repeating and recording the tossing, then the result starts to approach the 50/50 state that we know a fair coin should show. If a combination of valid merit and lottery was to be used repeatedly in life-changing events then perhaps we could approach a truly meritocratic state. The repeated use of lottery-choosing, especially weighted lotteries could finally produce the Meritocracy of equal outcomes to those of equal merit.

One inestimable virtue in such a system is that it draws the sting out of rejection. This is not intended to be a manifestation of trendy modern educational ideas where all must be winners, no-one can be branded a failure. But our current methods of selection when there are many more applicants than places must lead to repeated experiences of the psychologically damaging rejection and feelings of worthlessness. It is little comfort to re-assure the losers with bland platitudes of "you were good, but others were better". Rejection is rejection.

Theorists of decision-making like Savage recognised the greater impact that the experience of failure has compared to success. He designed a whole strategy around the 'no regret' principle. Psychologists too, gauge that failure can be three times or so more impacting than success. How much better then to be told that it was the impersonal mechanism of a lottery that decided your fate, rather than the human judgement of false merit based on interviews and the inspection of good works. Success in a lottery allocation of that prized educational place may not play into the conceit that you are uniquely meritorious, the best person who applied. But properly used, the lottery can turn the constant drizzle of rejection into something more bearable. That perhaps is the greatest contribution to human well-being that lottery-choosing could make.

Bibliography

Included here are published references such as books and papers in journals. Where I have found a story in a newspaper or on a website the source and date is given in the text, not in this section. Newspapers are British unless stated e.g. *The Times* is the London *Times*.

Atkinson, Adele; Gregg, Paul and McConnell, Brendon (2006) The result of 11 plus selection; An investigation into opportunities and outcomes for pupils in selective LEAs paper at CMPO Conference Bristol April 2006

Anand, Paul (2001) Procedural fairness in economic and social choice: Evidence from a survey of voters *J of Economic Psychology* 22 247-270

Angrist, Joshua (1990) Lifetime Earnings and the Vietnam Era Draft Lottery: Evidence from Social Security Administrative Records *The American Economic Review*, Vol. 80, No. 3. (Jun., 1990), pp. 313-336.)

Angrist, Joshua; Bettinger, Eric; Bloom, Erik; King, Elizabeth & Kremer, Michael (Dec, 2002) Vouchers for private schooling in Columbia: Evidence from a randomised natural experiment *American Economic Review* V92 No 5 1535-1558

Astin, Alexander W (1969, 21 Nov) Letter: Total View of Campus Unrest (1970, 20 Feb) Should College Applicants Be Selected by Lottery? in *Science*

Aubert, Vilhelm (1959) Chance in social affairs *Inquiry* 2(1) 1959 1-24

Ball, Michael (1988) *Rebuilding Construction* London; Routledge

Barnett, Anthony & Carty, Peter (1998) *The Athenian option: radical reform for the House of Lords* London: Demos. reprinted by Imprint Academic, Exeter 2008

Baron-Cohen, Simon (2003) *The essential difference: Men, women and the extreme male brain* London: AllenLane Penguin

Behrman, Jere; Sengupta, Piyali & Todd, Petra (2000) Progressing through PROGRESA: An impact assessment of Mexico's school subsidy program. Working paper, U of Pennsylvania and Int'l Food Policy Research Inst. http://pier.econ.upenn.edu/Archive/01-033.pdf

Bekhradnia, Bahram (2002) Who does best at university *HEFCE – Higher Education Funding Council for England* Bristol & London

Bekhradnia, Bahram (2003) Widening Participation and Fair Access: An Overview of the Evidence *HEPI –Higher Education Policy Institute* Oxford Feb 2003

Beynon, Huw & Austrin, Terry (1994) Masters and servants: Class and patronage in the making of a Labour organisation: The Durham miners and the English political tradition London: Rivers Oram Press

Bifulco R & Ladd H F (2007) School choice, racial segregation and test score gaps *J of policy Analysis* 26 (1) 31-56

Binmore, Ken & Klemper, Paul (2002) The biggest auction ever: The sale of British 3G telecom licences *The Economic Journal* 112 March 72-96

Boyle, Conall (1984) An expert system for valuation of residential properties *Journal of Valuation* 2 No 3 Spring

Boyle Conall (1998) Organizations selecting people: how the process could be made fairer by the appropriate use of lotteries *The Statistician* 47 Part 2, pp 291-321 London: Royal Statistical Society

Boyle, Conall (2006) *Who gets the prize: The case for random distribution in non-market allocation* M Phil thesis, University of Wales, Swansea

Brighouse, Harry *School Choice and Social Justice* (2000) Oxford University Press

Broome, John (1984) Uncertainty and fairness *The Economic Journal* 94 Sept 84 624-632

Broome, John (1984b) Selecting people randomly *Ethics* Oct 84 p38-55

Baumol, William J (1986) *Superfairness* Camb Mass M I T Press

Buchanan, James M (2003) *What is Public Choice Theory?* lecture given on 2nd Feb 2003 at Hillsdale College from http://www.hillsdale.edu/imprimis/ 2003/march/default.htm

Burgess, Simon; Ellen Greaves; Anna Vignoles & Deborah Wilson (2009a) What Parents Want: School preferences and school choice CMPO 09/222 Oct 2009

Burgess, Simon, Ellen Greaves, Anna Vignoles & Deborah Wilson (2009b) Parental choice of primary school in England: what 'type' of school do parents choose? November 2009Working Paper No. 09/224 Centre for Market and Public Organisation Bristol

Burnheim, John (1985) *Is democracy possible? The alternative to electoral politics* Cambridge UK Polity Press

Calabresi, Guido & Bobbitt, Philip (1978) *Tragic choices* NY: Norton

Callenbach, Ernest & Phillips, Michael (1985) *A Citizen Legislature A modest proposal for the random selection of legislators* Berkeley/Bodega, California

Cantillon, Estelle (2009) School Choice Procedures: How They Matter? Theory and Evidence from Belgium *paper at CMPO Bristol 9 June 2009 Conference* School choice in an international context: learning from other countries' experiences

Camerer, Colin (1995) Individual decision making; p 611-2 in Kagel, John H. & Roth, Alvin E. eds (1995). *The handbook of experimental economics*, Princeton: University Press

Carnevale, Anthony P & Rose, Stephen J (2003) *Socioeconomic status, race/ethnicity, and college admissions* New York, Century

Chomsky, Noam & Daly, Herman (1988) *Manufacturing Consent: The Political Economy of the Mass Media* Pantheon Books

Cohen-Schotanus Janke ; Muutjens Arno M. M. ; Reinders Janj ; Agstreibbe Jessica ; Van Rossum Herman T. M. ; van der Vleuten Cees P. M. ; (2006) The predictive validity of grade point average scores in a partial lottery medical school admission system *Medical education* 2006, vol. 40, n°10, pp. 1012-1019 Blackwell, Oxford, UK

Cullen, Julie Berry; Jacob, Brian A & Levitt, Steven (Nov 2003) The effect of school choice on student outcomes: Evidence from randomized lotteries. NBER Working Paper 10113

Dawes, R. M. (1971)0 A case study of graduate admissions: Application of three principles of human decision making *American Psychologist*, vol. 26, pp. 180–8.

DCSF (Department for Children, Schools and Families) (2009) *School Admissions Code 2009 Edition* London; The Stationery Office

Department for Education and Skills (27 April 2006) *School Admission Code – Draft Skeleton* London; The Stationery Office

DeWitt L B (1971). A lottery system for higher education. Notes on the Future of Education, volume 2 issue 3, summer 1971, 9-12. A publication of the Educational policy Research Center at Syracuse

Dowlen, Oliver (2008) *The Political Potential of Sortition*. Exeter: Imprint Academic

Drenth, P. J. D. (voorzitter) (1997) *Gewogen loting gewogen. Advies van de Commissie Toelating Numerus Fixusopleidingen.* Met Bijlage. Zoetermeer: Ministerie van Onderwijs, Cultuur en Wetenschappen / Den Haag: Sdu Servicecentrum

Drenth, P J D (1999) The selection of medical students in the Netherlands – Reconciling the incompatibles *Commission on the Points System*

Research Paper No 3 Department of Education, Dublin: Irish Government

Dunn, Elizabeth W. ; Timothy D. Wilson & Daniel T. Gilbert (2003) Location, Location, Location: The Mis-prediction of Satisfaction in Housing Lotteries *Personality and Social Psychology Bulletin*, Vol. 29, No. 11, 1421-1432 (2003)

Duxbury, Neil (1999) *Random justice - on lotteries and legal decision-making* Oxford, Clarendon Press

Edgeworth, F Y (1888) The statistics of examinations *J Roy Stat Soc* London 51 599-635

Edgeworth, F Y (1890) The element of chance in competitive examinations *J Roy Stat Soc* London 53 644-663

Education and Skills Committee (2004)*Secondary Education: School Admissions Fourth Report of Session 2003–04* http://www.publications. parliament.uk/pa/cm200304/cmselect/cmeduski/58/5802.htm

Elster, Jon (1989). *Solomonic judgements: studies in the limitations of rationality*, Cambridge: University Press

Estache, Antonio; Laffont, Jean-Jacques & Zhang, Xinzhu (2004) Downsizing with labor sharing and collusion *Journal of Development Economics* 73 (2004) 519– 540

Eysenck, H J (1962) *Know your own I.Q.* Harmondsworth: Penguin

Fang Lai (2007) The effect of winning a first-choice school entry lottery on student performance: evidence from a natural experiment; New York University http://www.ncspe.org/publications_files/OP139.pdf

Fehr, Ernst & Schmidt, Klaus M(2001) Theories of fairness and reciprocity: Evidence and economic application: Discussion paper 2001-2, Department of Economics, University of Munich

Ferguson, Eamonn; David James, Laura Madeley (2002) Factors associated with success in medical school: systematic review of the literature *BMJ* 2002;324:952–7

Fienberg, S. E. (1973), Randomization for the Selective Service Draft Lotteries, in *Statistics by Example: Finding Models*, eds. F. Mosteller, W. H. Kruskal, R. F. Link, R. S. Pieters, & G. R. Rising, Reading, MA: Addison-Wesley, pp. 1-13

Finlay, Robert (1980) *Politics in Renaissance Venice* London: Ernest Benn

Fox, Dov (2004) The Truth about Harvard: A Behind the Scenes Look at Admissions and Life on Campus *The Princeton Review*, 2004

Frank, Robert H (2004) *What price the moral high ground? Ethical dilemmas in competitive environments* Princeton: University Press

Friedman, Milton (1995) Public Schools: Make Them Private; published by the Cato Institute at http://www.cato.org/pubs /briefs /bp-023.html

Gataker, Thomas (1627) *The Nature and Uses of Lotteries: A Historical and Theological Treatise Historical* Modernised with Notes and Bibliography by Boyle, Conall (2008) Exeter: Imprint Academic

Gibbons, S. & S. Machin, (2006) Paying for primary schools: Supply constraints, school popularity or congestion, *Economic Journal*, 116 (510): C77-C92 March 2006

Gibbons, S. & S. Machin (2007) Valuing School Quality, Better Transport and Lower Crime: Evidence from House Prices *Oxford Review of Economic Policy Housing Markets Seminar at Saïd Business School* 12/9/07

Gipps, C & Murphy, P (1994) *A fair test? Assessment achievement and equity* Buckingham: O U Press

Goodwin, Barbara (2007 5e) *Using political ideas*, John Wiley Chichester

Goodwin, Barbara (2005 2e) *Justice by lottery* Exeter: Imprint Academic

Goudappel, Flora (1999) The Dutch system of lottery for studies *European Journal for Education Law and Policy* Volume 3, Number 1 / March, 1999

Greely, Hank (1977) The equality of allocation by lot *Harvard Civil Rights Civil Liberties Law Review* 12 1 1977

Grofman, Bernard & Merill, Samuel (2004) Anticipating Likely Consequences of Lottery-Based Affirmative Action *Social Science Qly*, Vol 85, Number 5, December 2004

Guinier, Lani (2002) *The Miner's Canary: Enlisting Race, Resisting Power, & Transforming Democracy* Harvard University Press

Haddad, Moussa (2004) *School Admissions: A Report of the* Social Market Foundation London (July 2004) Moussa Haddad (Ed.)

Haspel, Abraham E. (1990) Drilling for Dollars: The new and improved federal oil-lease program Regulation *American enterprise institute journal of government and society* July/Aug 1985

Hastings, Justine S; Kane, Thomas J & Staiger, Douglas O (2006) Gender and Performance: Evidence from School Assignment by Randomized Lottery NBER paper

Herbst, Susan (1998) *Reading Public Opinion: How political actors view the political process* Chicago University Press

Herrnstein, Richard J & Murray, Charles (1994) *Bell Curve: Intelligence and Class Structure in American Life* Glencoe, Illinois, Free Press

Hicks, Gary (2009) *Fate's Bookie: How the lottery shaped the world* Stroud, Gloucestershire, The History Press

Hofstee, W. K. B., & Trommar, P. M. (1976) Selectie en Loting: Meningen van VWO-Eindexaminandi. Heymans Bulletin, No. 25 1, Department of Psychology, University of Groningen.

Hofstee, Willem K B (1983) The Case for Compromise in Educational Selection and Grading In Scarvia B. Anderson & John S. Helmick (Eds) *On educational testing*. San Francisco: Jossey-Bass Publishers. p. 109-127.

Hofstee, Willem K B (1990) Allocation by lot: a conceptual and empirical analysis *Rationality and Society* **29 4** Dec 745-763

Howell, William G.; Wolf, Patrick J.; Peterson, Paul E. & Campbell, David E. (2000) Test-Score Effects of School Vouchers in Dayton, New York, and Washington: Evidence from Randomized Field Trials. Paper presented at the annual meeting of the American Political Science Association, Washington, DC, Sept 2000. http://www.hks.harvard.edu/pepg/PDF/Papers/dnw00x.pdf

Hylland, Aanund; Richard Zeckhauser (1979) The Efficient Allocation of Individuals to Positions *The Journal of Political Economy*, Vol. 87, No. 2. (Apr., 1979), pp. 293-314

Jacobs, Lesley A (2003) *Pursuing Equal Opportunities: The Theory and Practice of Egalitarian Justice*. New York: Cambridge University Press.

Jarvis, Helen; Alvanides, Seraphim (2008) School choice from a household resource perspective: Preliminary findings from a north of England case study *Community, Work & Family*, Volume 11, Number 4, November 2008 , pp. 385-403(19)

Jencks, Christopher & Meredith Phillips, eds. (1998). The Black-White Test Score Gap. Washington, DC: Brookings Institution Press.

Kahneman D & Tversky A (1979) Prospect theory: an analysis of decision under risk. *Econometrica* 47 pp. 263–291.

Kahneman, Daniel (2003) A psychological perspective on economics *American Economic Review v*92, no 2 163-168

Karbel, Jerome (2005) *The Chosen: The Hidden History of Admission and Exclusion at Harvard, Yale, and Princeton* New York; Houghton Mifflin Harcourt

Kelman E G & Canger S (1994) Validity of Interviews for Admissions Evaluation *J of Veterinary Medical Education* v21n2

Kline, Paul (1991) *Intelligence: The psychometric view* London, Routledge

Klitgaard, Robert (1985) *Choosing elites* New York, Basic Books

Kreiter Clarence D; Yin Ping; Solow Catherine; Brennan Robert L Investigating the reliability of the medical school admissions interview. *Advances in health sciences education : theory and practice* 2004;9(2):147-59

Krueger, Alan B. & Zhu, Pei (2003). Another Look at the New York City School Voucher Experiment. National Bureau of Economic Research, Working Paper 9418.

Lavy

Lavy, Victor (2006) From Forced Busing to Free Choice in Public Schools: Quasi-Experimental Evidence of Individual and General Effects, NBER Working Paper No. 11969 January 2006

Leech, Dennis & Campos, Erick (2003) Is comprehensive education really free?: a case-study of the effects of secondary school admissions policies on house prices in one local area *Journal Of The Royal Statistical Society Series A*, 2003, vol. 166, 1, 135-154

Le Grand, Julian (21 Feb 2006), The Blair Legacy? Choice and Competition in Public Services Transcript of Public Lecture London School of Economics which can be found at http://www.lse.ac.uk/ collections/ LSEPublicLecturesAndEvents/pdf/20060221-LeGrand.pdf

Levitt, Steven D. & Dubner, Stephen J. (2005) *Freakonomics: A Rogue Economist Explores the Hidden Side of Everything* Allan Lane: London, followed by *Superfreakonomics* (2009).

Lobe, Kenton & Berkes, Firket (2004) A *padu* system of community-based fisheries management: change and local institutional innovation in South India *Marine Policy* 28 271-278

Matloff, Norman (1995) Why not a lottery to get into UC? The pool of academically eligible students would be diversified, meeting affirmative action, ending abuse, *Los Angeles Times* Jan 24, 1995

Mankiw, N. Gregory (1999) Economics First Principles: Vouchers: Schools Need Competition *Fortune* June 7, 1999 available at: http://www.economics.harvard.edu/files/faculty/40_june799.html

Montgomery, Douglas C (2008 6e) *Introduction to Statistical Quality Control* Wiley; New York

Neave, Henry (1990) *The Deming dimension* Knoxville Tenn S P C Press

Oberholzer-Gee, Felix; Bohnet, Iris & Frey, Bruno (1997) Fairness and competence in democratic decisions *Public Choice* 91 89-105

O'Hear, A (2007) Editorial: The Equality Lottery , *Philosophy* 82, No. 2 (April 2007), 209–10

Parkinson, C Northcote (1958) *Parkinson's law or the pursuit of progress* London John Murray

Patterson, F., Lane, P., Ferguson, E., & Norfolk, T. (2001). Competency based selection system for general practitioner registrars. *BMJ Careers*, 323(2), 1-6.

Perry, Orit ; Erev, Ido & Haruvy, Ernan (2001) Frequent probabalistic punishment in law enforcement *Economics of Governance* own pub http://www2.gsb.columbia.edu/faculty/ierev/pages/red.pdf

Peterson, Paul E (2002). Victory for Vouchers? *Commentary.* 114 (2): 46-51

Queller, Donald E & Swietek, Francis R (1977) Two studies on Venetian Government; *Etudes de Philosophe et Histoire* Geneve, Librarie Droz

Rawls, John (1972) *A Theory of Justice* Oxford University Press

Roth, Alvin E (2002) The economist as engineer: Game theory, experimentation, and computation as tools for design economics *Economica* 70 1341-1378

Rothstein, Jesse (2009) Teacher Quality in Educational Production: Tracking, Decay, and Student Achievement NBER paper

Rouse, C E (1997) Private School Vouchers and Student Achievement: An Evaluation of the Milwaukee Parental Choice Program NBER Working Paper No. 5964

Sacerdote, Bruce (2000) Peer effects with random assignments: Results for Dartmouth roommates, *The Quarterly Journal of Economics* V 116 No: 2 P: 681 – 704, May 2001

Samaha, Adam M (2008) Randomization in Adjudication: The University of Chicago Law School Paper (privately circulated paper)

Saunders, Ben (2008) The equality of lotteries *Philosophy* 83 359–372

Schwartz, Steven (2004a). *Fair admissions to higher education: recommendations and good practice*, Admissions to Higher Education Steering Group, Nottingham: Department for Education and Skills Publications, available at www.admissions-review.org.uk

Schwartz, Steven (2004b) evidence to Commons Select Cttee: Admissions to Higher Education --pdf http://www.parliament.the-stationery-office.co.uk/pa/cm200405/cmselect/cmeduski/uc41-i/uc4101.htm 25 Nov 2004

Simpson, M. A. (1975). Selection of medical students by lottery. *Journal of Medical Education*, 50, 417-418

Slater, Helen; Davies, Neil & Burgess, Simon (2009) Do teachers matter? Measuring the variation in teacher effectiveness in England Working Paper No. 09/212 *Centre for Market and Public Organisation* Bristol University

Stone, Peter (2007) Why lotteries are just *J. of Political Philosophy* 15 no. 3 (Sept 2007): 276-295

Stone, Peter. (2008) What Can Lotteries Do for Education? *Theory and Research in Education* 6, no 3 (November 2008): 267-282

Stone, Peter (2009) Lotteries, Education and Opportunity unpub

Stone, Peter (2010) The good, the right and the random Presentation at the 2010 Annual Meeting of the Western Political Science Association

Stone *Luck of the Draw* (forthcoming)

Suen, Wing & Tang, Bo-Sin (1984) Optimal site area for high-density housing development The University of Hong Kong; *Economics Letters* 15, 189-193

Sutherland, Keith (2004) *The Party's Over: Blueprint for a very English revolution* Exeter, Imprint Academic

Sutton Research Trust (May 2007) Ballots in school admissions; from http://www.suttontrust.com/annualreports.asp

Taylor, Howard F (1980) *The IQ game: A methodological inquiry into the heredity-environment controversy* New Brunswick NJ: Rutgers U P

Taylor, Grant A.,Tsui, Kevin K K. & Zhu, Lijing (May 2003) *Lottery or waiting-line auction?* J Public Economics Elsevier

ten Cate, Th. J. & H. L. Hendrix (2001). De eerste ervaringen met selectie voor de artsopleiding. *Nederlands Tijdschrift voor Geneeskunde, 145*, 1364-1368

Tough, Sarah; Brooks, Richard (2007) *School admissions: Fair choice for parents and pupils* IPPR Institute for Public Policy Research www.ippr.org London

Traub, James (2005) Ivory tower intrigues; the pseudo-meritocracy of the Ivy league *Slate* Oct 24, 2005 http://www.slate.com/id/2128377/ This is part of a review of Karbel, Jerome (2005) *The Chosen: The Hidden History of Admission and Exclusion at Harvard, Yale, and Princeton* Houghton Mifflin

Urlings-Strop, Louise C, Stijnen, Theo, Themmen, Axel P N & Splinter, Ted A W (2009) Selection of medical students: a controlled experiment *Medical Education* Blackwell Publishing Ltd V 43; 2 175-183

Vernon, P E ed (1957) *Secondary school selection: A British Psychological Society Inquiry* London: Methuen

Vernooij, Meike W. M.D., M. Arfan Ikram, M.D., Hervé L. Tanghe, M.D., Arnaud J.P.E. Vincent, M.D., Albert Hofman, M.D ., Gabriel P. Krestin, M.D., Wiro J. Niessen, Ph.D., Monique M.B. Breteler, M.D., & Aad van der Lugt, M.D. (2007) Incidental Findings on Brain MRI in the General Population *New England Journal of Medicine* 2007, 357:1821-8

Young, Michael (1958) *The rise of Meritocracy 1870-2033: An essay on education and equality* London Thames & Hudson

Wainwright, Martin (2007) *The Guardian Book of April Fool's Day* London, Aurum Press

Witte, J.F. (1997). Achievement Effects of the Milwaukee Voucher Program. American Economics Association Annual Meeting, New Orleans.

Wolfle, Dael (1970) Chance, or Human Judgment? Editorial in *Science* 27 Feb 1970, V167, 3922 p1201

Zwick, Rebecca. (2002) *Fair Game? The Use of Standardized Admissions Tests in Higher Education.* New York/London. Routledge Falmer

Index